INCREASING PRODUCTIVITY AND SALES

William L. Kahrl

Managing for Profit Series

Lebhar-Friedman Books
Chain Store Publishing Corp.
A Subsidiary of Lebhar-Friedman Inc.
New York

Increasing Productivity and Sales
Managing for Profit Series

Copyright © 1980, Chain Store Publishing Corp.,
425 Park Avenue, New York, N.Y. 10022

All rights reserved. No part of this book is to be reproduced in any form or by any means without permission in writing from the publisher.

Printed in the United States of America
Library of Congress Catalog Card Number: 80-81944
ISBN: 0-912016-41-8

5 4 3 2 1

TX
911.3
.L27
K34

CONTENTS

Foreword vii
Introduction 1
PRODUCTIVITY IN FOOD SERVICE 9
Increasing Productivity 18
Steps for Increasing Productivity 20
INTERRELATION OF SALES AND PRODUCTIVITY 43
FOOD SERVICE SALES 47
New Emphasis on Selling 47
Measuring Sales 49
Sales Analysis 58
Increasing Sales 60
SUMMARY 91

APPENDIX 95

FOREWORD

A series of manuals has been prepared for the food service industry by William L. Kahrl, author of *Planning and Operating a Successful Food Service Operation* and *Meeting Challenges in Food Service:* a guide for solving present and future problems. Each manual deals with a specific problem area common to all segments of the industry, offering solutions and serving as a training aid for management, key personnel, and their employees.

The food service industry is comprised of twenty-five or more segments, each with its own variations. Experience has taught us, however, that despite such diversity, there are problem areas common to all. Furthermore, the functions of good planning, tight controls, proper service of food, and cleanliness can be associated with all segments of the industry. So each of the problem areas discussed and its associated principles should find application throughout all segments of the food service industry.

Experience in analyzing many facilities over the years has also taught that the best way to solve a large problem is to break it down into smaller parts that can be carefully studied and corrected until the whole problem has been solved. As in medicine, diagnosis precedes cure; a series of manuals has been prepared to assist you in your diagnosis and cure of many of the ills that sap the profit and progress of your industry.

INTRODUCTION

As the food service industry continues to grow larger and becomes a more important part of many people's lives, more and more time and effort is being devoted to improve the industry, make it more efficient, and of course more profitable. Almost every American will eat one out of two meals away from home and the industry is now employing some eight million people. It is time for it to "grow up" and take its place as one of the leaders in the country. I will soon have spent 50 years in the food service industry and have seen and experienced a great many changes. We have battled our way through a major depression, quite a few wars, recessions, boom times, and inflation. Through it all the industry just keeps growing. Now, more and more people are forced to eat away from home. Even greater numbers choose to eat out, as more women work outside the home and our society places greater emphasis on leisure time and travel.

Not only has the growth been fast, but it has caught many by surprise. The early days of food service were marked by the "mom/pop" type operation; few ever dreamed of the huge chains that would emerge. According to the *Nation's Restaurant News* Chain Analysis (August 6, 1979), the 100 top volume food service chains accounted for 31 percent of total U.S. food service sales ($101 billion). As of July 1, 1979, the chains are growing fast not only in number but in percent of the total food service sales. However, this still leaves most of the business being done by the individual operator and the many thousands of small facilities. The food service industry is one of few major industries where an individual can start his/her own business on a shoestring and still make it. However, as investment prices and costs of doing business rise, it is becoming more and more difficult for the individual operator which explains why the large chains continue to grow and capture more and more of the market.

This situation may also explain the low productivity in the food service industry. Not too many years ago the productivity in food service was so low in comparison to other retail industries that the federal government took note of it and set up some special task forces to determine the causes and suggest some remedies. The national commission on productivity reported virtually zero productivity growth from 1964 to 1971 for the food service industry. Early in the nineteen-seventies employees in service restaurants in this country were responsible for $13,500 a year in sales each. Four or five years later this had risen to $19,000 per year per employee, but a closer look showed that the industry's productivity had not increased; it only was the large increases in menu prices that had increased the sales and the apparent productivity. No doubt the sales per employee have risen again, but this is due primarily to the continuing high menu price increases and does not reflect increased efficiency or productivity. Inflationary periods can lull people into a false sense that they are doing a much better job. Just look how sales and productivity are increasing! We must be doing a better job and getting to be more efficient! About the only thing many in the industry have improved is their ability to raise menu prices. In light of all that has happened to the food service industry, it will certainly pay to take another very close look at productivity. Sure we can achieve some moderately high productivity figures with excessively high menu prices, but what would happen if menu prices had to be cut back? Could the facility producing in excess of $1 million a year in gross sales with a $3.00 check average produce the same sales as we were forced to do back in the late nineteen-thirties with a 50 cent check average? Perhaps we haven't progressed as much as we should have over the years.

The study of economics has shown that, in general, there are cycles of ups and downs. What goes down must eventually come up and what goes up must go down (at least this is the way it is supposed to happen, although there are times when this seems not to work at all). In short, nothing lasts forever and the smart business owner plans ahead for the time when conditions will be different. Shortly after World War II, our industry really started to grow. We were still enjoying an ample supply of cheap help and only a very few in the industry realized that the day would come when waiters/waitresses would have to be paid, wages would increase, and the free ride would be over. Some work was done in the fifties to improve efficiency and productivity, but it was not widespread or significant. Then in the sixties and seventies the menu price increases started and once again we were on a "free" ride. Why worry about making studies, doing research, and cutting waste and inefficiency? Just keep raising menu prices and sit and enjoy the profits without too much exertion. Prices in all categories—fast food, family restaurants, and gourmet—have already exceeded the top figures thought possible by many, and the increases keep going. However, there may be some dark clouds on the horizon, as indicated by the lead article in *Nation's Restaurant News* (August 6, 1979):

Soaring menu prices erode sales: economic uncertainties, energy cloud future for many operators
By Charles Bernstein

Menu prices soared an average of 11.15% for the five months ended during the first half of the year, compared with the same period the previous year. This industrywide figure probably matched the price rises registered by many of the top 100 chains, faced with skyrocketing costs.

The net effect has been definite customer resistance and customer erosions. Although the necessity for continued rapid menu price increases may be alleviated in the second half and during 1980, the threat of a recession raises just as serious a problem.

Few of the leading chains were able to outdistance the average 11% menu price hike figure in their comparative unit volumes this year. And the per-square-foot productivity figures show even smaller increases since most of the newer units are larger and should generate proportionately bigger volumes.

Economic uncertainties cloud the immediate future—gas shortages, the entire energy crisis and a recession in particular. There are no easy answers to these dilemmas, but methods of raising the average unit volumes faster will have to be found.

Major chains which did manage to top the 11% average sales increase barrier this year were Gino's, Hardee's and Burger Chef, each up 12%; Burger King and A&W, each up 16%; Taco Bell, 14%; International Dairy Queen, 17%; Howard Johnson, 18%, and Bonanza, 15%.

The first three all showed slow growth previously and had a considerable distance to climb back. But Gino's, Hardee's and Burger Chef climbed much faster this year than in the previous year. This may be related to menu add-ons to lessen dependence on the burger.

A&W, in the midst of a rebuilding program, still has a $215,000 average unit volume. Burger King, though, is actually outpacing the 10% annual sales growth goal set by parent Pillsbury.

Biggest disappointments in the burger fast-food segment were McDonald's, up 7% in average unit volume; Wendy's, up 4%, and Jack in the Box, up 3%. The first two chains are still showing formidable figures, but at a declining rate. They simply haven't been able to resist the pressures on beef costs and prices.

Taco Bell, owned by PepsiCo, has modernized many of its units and has spread into some bigger population areas in the East. IDQ has continued to expand its menu with more selections while Howard Johnson's escalation is due primarily to the increased emphasis on Ground Round restaurants in neighborhoods and shopping centers.

Bonanza's 15% surge is pegged to the fact that it is now almost entirely franchised and that, as the chain's executives had predicted, the franchisees are scoring higher volumes.

Among the more disappointing performances were those of Pizza Hut, up only 5% despite an all-out effort by parent PepsiCo; Denny's, with a 3% increase and a slower growth; Sambo's, believed to be down slightly in its average volume, and Victoria Station, staying about the same. (Again, these figures were achieved in units that were, on the average, larger and carried higher investment costs.)

Prospects are that the almost 8% new unit expansion rate envisioned by the top 100 chains will have to be scaled down to concentrate more on a push for maximum unit volumes.

The 11.15 percent average increase for menu prices in the first five months of 1979 has caused definite customer resistance and customer count erosions.

Once customer resistance puts an end to the menu price increases, and we lose the cheap labor market as well, the food service industry will be forced to seek other means to stay in business and make a profit. When both of these "easy way out" solutions (cheap labor and higher selling prices) that we have relied on for so many years are gone, someone must do some real studying and planning for the future. This should mark the start of better times for consultants and for those in our industry who did look ahead and realize the "free rides" had to end some time. The low productivity, high employee turnover, and inability to pay the going wage rates that have so long been characteristic of the industry must be changed to put us in a more favorable position. Smart operators know that there are always changes and problems to be met. They plan ahead so that they can gradually adapt their businesses to existing conditions. However, many of us wait until the last minute, push the panic button, and dash around looking for another quick and easy way out. Will the federal government bail us out of our troubles next time?

If one side of the profit coin is productivity, then the other side is sales. Of course, everyone knows all there is to know about sales—at the end of the day you push the total button on your cash register and there it is: total dollar sales or meals sold for the day. In seven days you have the total for the week, and it accumulates until you arrive at gross yearly sales. If you have to increase sales then raise the menu prices again, run an ad in the local paper, put a "special" sign in the window, or increase the TV advertising and your problems are solved. Why bother to analyze the sales figures to find out how we are doing? It seems very simple. Many don't realize that:

- It is possible to increase sales and make a smaller profit
- It is possible to decrease sales and make a greater profit
- It is possible to lower selling prices and increase sales
- It is possible to increase sales and lose customers
- It is possible to increase selling prices and decrease sales
- It is possible to increase productivity without increasing sales
- It is possible to increase sales and not increase productivity
- It is possible to lower prices and make a greater profit

If all the above assumptions are true (and they are possible), then there is more to sales figures than just pushing that button on the register and getting a total reading.

This whole picture of increasing productivity and sales deserves a closer look; that is exactly what we are going to do in this book. Not only will we explore the many ways to increase productivity and sales, but we will try to explain what the various figures you should be getting mean and how and when to take action once you have understood the figures. By now, with computers and all the other accounting aids we have, there are an abundance of reports, figures, charts, and graphs to help the food service industry. However, if people do not look at these figures and reports, fail to understand what they mean, and take no remedial action when they see the danger signals, then all of this costly effort is for nothing except to tell you "you have just gone broke!" That latest report you are quickly glancing over shows your sales have increased. Just great! But does that mean that everything is going well and you have nothing to worry about? Let's look again:

    Was the increase due to recent menu price increases?
    Will the customer count hold or decrease?
    Was the increase due to those three new units you just opened?
    Have unit sales in existing operations decreased?
    Were the increased sales due to that big special and expensive TV promotion you know you can't afford?
    Was the sales increase the regular seasonal increase and was it more or less than last year's?

Perhaps this is a pessimistic attitude and we should just accept the increased sales and be happy.

However, just as it is important to know why *costs* have increased or decreased, it is just as important to know what caused the *sales* increases.

The reasons for increased or decreased cost must also be examined. I can walk into any food service operation, immediately slash costs to make a good impression, and produce a temporary increase in profits:

    Cut the staff and temporarily put more load on the rest of the employees
    Cut quality of food purchased
    Reduce food portions
    Stop all expenditures for advertising

Stop all preventive maintenance
Cut back on cleaning and sanitation
Cut all inventories and purchases to the bone
Include the depreciation allowances in profits

Although the above moves aren't very wise and will seriously hurt a food service operation in the long run, they will produce quick cost reductions and profit increases. This has been done many times in the past and is still being done by those who want to make a good quick impression or squeeze out all the profit possible as a speculator. For example, everyone in the business charges off amortization and depreciation each year as an expense allowable by the Internal Revenue Service. Half of the amount entered this way should be held as a reserve, so that when the time comes to replace that old worn-out equipment or fix the building, the money will be there. This can amount to 3 percent or more of the total sales depending on the operation. Many, however, look at this as part of the profit each year. "I only made 5 percent net last year, but I charged off 5 percent depreciation so actually I made 10 percent net!" Great idea and very impressive, but when that equipment wears out and you have no money for a replacement, then what? It just so happens that trying to operate with obsolete equipment and outdated layouts is one of the food service industry's biggest problems today in the area of productivity. The new equipment is available to help do a better job, but if you don't have the money to buy it, then you must struggle along with the old and the resulting high repair and maintenance costs.

If you are a bit confused at this point, do not be discouraged. Your admission that you are a bit confused and don't know all the answers means that you are one of the smart ones who will take the time to better understand what is happening and to decide what to do about it. The scriptures repeatedly rebuke those who "have eyes to see and see not . . . ears to hear and hear not." This certainly applies to us now as well. The signs and figures are all there; we have made the studies and devised countless measures to solve our problems, but if we can't see or hear them, then little can be done to help. We know that in the vast majority of cases we need increased sales to improve the profit picture, but unfortunately we are still looking for that easy way out. Some of the other solutions are not all that difficult, but they will take a little time and effort.

PRODUCTIVITY IN FOOD SERVICE

Food service is one of the very few retail industries where manufacturing and selling take place in the same premise or building. Most retail industries are sharply divided, with one segment doing the manufacturing and the other engaging in sales only. This clear distinction makes for a much more efficient and productive total operation, as is evidenced by the sales per employee per year figures of these industries. We are still bringing raw products in the back, preparing, cooking, and then selling the finished product out front. This is the equivalent of shoe stores making the shoes on display in the back room. Retail sales outlets don't operate this way. Almost all of them now engage and concentrate on selling only, leaving the manufacturing to others. Imagine the problem of a modern drug store trying to make all the items they have for sale in the back room! The more items the food service operation has for sale and the more items made or manufactured in the back, the more difficult the job becomes.

Many years ago, America made use of the assembly line and automation to become the industrial leader of the world. We discovered new systems and methods to mass-produce products while other nations were still struggling with the old systems. Some say that we gave up quality, but we did raise the standard of living, making it possible for most Americans to enjoy products like cars and TV. It is time for food service to look at new ways to fulfill its function with new methods and technology.

One definition of productivity is the "ability to bring forth; make or manufacture." Productivity in food service can be measured several different ways. The accounting methods ordinarily used have little bearing on productivity because these figures do not show up in profit and loss statements or balance sheets. These measures can be:

Dollar sales per man hour (or week, month, etc.)
Meals per man hour
Dollar sales per employee per year

In institutional feeding (schools, hospitals, etc.) where dollar amounts do not enter into the picture except for costs, we can get productivity figures using meals served. The industry as a whole, and the government when it makes a comparative study, use the dollar or meal per employee per year. Earlier it was mentioned that the sales per employee per year in the early seventies was $13,500 for service restaurants. Four or five years later this increased to $19,000, which would have indicated that the industry became more productive, but when adjustments were made for price increases, we still had the same old zero productivity growth.

There are other measurements you can use. Some years ago I made a six-month study of school lunch programs. Some schools had systems that served only about six students per minute, while other more modern setups were moving 15 students per minute through the lines. Certainly this is also a measure of productivity; if you are serving only six students per minute and someone else is serving 15, there is something wrong with your system.

Calculating these productivity figures is not a difficult job. Let's start with a weekly basis. Most operations pay on this basis, which means they keep a weekly schedule and payroll sheet. A carefully kept record of sales will give you the total dollar sales for the week. Your weekly payroll sheet shows individual and total hours worked plus wage rates. Total weekly sales divided by total man hours equals sales per man hour. Total meals served in a week divided by total man hours equals meals served per man hour. This figure can be quickly checked with the previous week or year to give you an idea of your progress. The best way to explain this is to use an example:

Restaurant XXX has approximately $420,000 in yearly sales. The week we are checking is an average one, with $8,000 total sales, $2,080 total payroll, and 533 total man hours.

Sales per Man Hour Needed to Produce Certain Wage Percent of Sales

Average Hourly Wage Rate	24%	25%	26%	27%	28%	29%
3.50	14.58	14.00	13.46	12.96	12.50	12.07
3.60	15.00	14.40	13.85	13.33	12.86	12.41
3.70	15.42	14.80	14.23	13.70	13.21	12.76
3.80	15.83	15.20	14.62	14.07	13.57	13.10
3.90	16.25	15.60	15.00	14.44	13.93	13.45
4.00	16.67	16.00	15.38	14.81	14.29	13.79
4.10	17.08	16.40	15.77	15.19	14.64	14.14
4.20	17.50	16.80	16.15	15.60	15.00	14.48
4.30	17.92	17.20	16.54	16.30	15.71	15.17
4.40	18.33	17.60	16.92	16.30	15.71	15.17
4.50	18.75	18.00	17.31	16.67	16.07	15.52
4.60	19.17	18.40	17.69	17.04	16.43	15.86
4.70	19.58	18.80	18.08	17.41	16.79	16.21
4.80	20.00	19.20	18.46	17.78	17.14	16.55

Total sales of $8,000 divided by 533 man hours equals $15.00/man hour.
Total payroll of $2,080 divided by 533 man hours equals $3.90 average hourly wage rate.

If we examine the standard chart for sales per man hour needed to produce a certain wage percent of sales and go to the column of 26 percent, which is the wage cost we are hoping to make, we find that with an average hourly wage rate of $3.90 we should be producing $15.00 sales per man hour, so we are exactly on course. If our sales drop to $7,500 the next week and the payroll figures remain the same, our sales per man hour will be only $14.00. Checking our chart again we find that this will jump our percent wage cost to almost 28 percent for this week: 2 percent higher than our budget calls for. We must either bring the sales up again or cut the total man hours in the coming week. If the sales remain at $7,500 then we must cut the total man hours from 533 to 500 to maintain our 26 percent wage cost. Naturally the best course of action is to increase sales and productivity, which will lower our percentage of costs and produce more profit. Anyone with a small pocket calculator and a few minutes each week can determine these simple figures and know exactly where the business stands. Once this procedure is started and the records are kept, it will be easy to spot trouble quickly and make minor adjustments fast to stay on course.
What can these productivity figures do for you and your business?

Wasted Man Hours

Productivity figures can tell you at the end of each week if you have wasted man hours and exactly how many. Because many in our industry have long hours of operation (15 to 24 hours a day, seven days a week) we can have a lot of wasted man hours. Most food service operations are busy only during meal times or about 30 percent of the time they are open. The man hours wasted when the store is not busy can never be recovered and are a total loss. In the example given earlier, when the sales dropped from $8,000 to $7,500 for the week, we had 33 wasted man hours. If the sales continue at this lower level and these 33 wasted man hours aren't eliminated, the wage cost will end up 2 percent higher than normal and the profit 2 percent lower. This is a very simple explanation of the problem and solution, but it does point out how these figures can help locate and solve the trouble. Cutting 33 hours isn't as simple as cutting one full-time 40 hour/week employee. It will involve rearranging hours in the part-time area. The sales/hour figures for your operation can help in this instance, because with this record you can tell at just what times the business has decreased, and concentrate on these specific times. If the business has dropped during the breakfast time, then you must either try to build this back up, or cut some man hours during those morning hours.

Efficiency of Layout

If your productivity figures are consistently lower than those of similar operations, and you have tried several minor adjustments to improve them, it could be that your layout and equipment are outdated and not suited to modern food service. One of the main factors contributing to low productivity in food service is the great number of old facilities with badly worn equipment that makes it hard to operate efficiently. These places are usually large, were designed for a large staff of cooks, servers, etc., and have little or no automated or labor-saving equipment. They were built for an entirely different era and kind of food service operation; in short, they were designed for a time when all costs were low and there was plenty of cheap labor. Trying to operate and compete with these places is like trying to win today's Indianapolis "500" race with an old Stutz Bearcat or Model T Ford. Several years ago I was called in to check the food service facilities of a hotel over 50 years old that was still trying to operate with the *same* equipment it had started with. What I saw was unbelievable, but it illustrates what many are trying to do. We know from studies that our employees spend 25 to 30 percent of their time on the job walking when they could be standing still and producing. If your layout and equipment don't fit your menus, employees, or the type of place you are trying to run, then you could have wasted a lot of man hours and motion that will never be recovered. This will be discussed in detail later in the book.

Employee Capability

With the food service industry's record of low wages and unskilled labor, there can be little doubt that many of our employees are not capable of high productivity. Most enter our industry with little or no experience, they receive poor indoctrination and training, and don't stay on the job long enough to become productive. Anyone who eats out regularly can relate numerous bad experiences in restaurants and other food service establishments—poor service is one of the major complaints from customers. This explains why so many places are changing to a very simple menu and service. The steak, baked potato, and salad bar in many instances is not the most profitable menu to serve, but it requires little skill on the part of employees either in food preparation or serving.

There is a strange paradox here: as menu prices keep going up and up, customers naturally expect better food and service for their money. However, to a greater and greater extent the food service industry must work with unskilled employees who are not capable of producing this level of food and service. The menu prices keep going up, the waiting lines become longer, the employees less productive, and the customer complaints even louder.

It is not easy to change a situation like this overnight. As we all know, more training is needed, but if you can't attract the kind of people who are willing to stay on the job and learn, training becomes a difficult task. The answer is in offering better wages to attract better people to start with. If these new employees can be enticed to make food service a career and stay on the job, then we will be able to build a force of trained, capable employees. This is why productivity is so important to any industry. If your employees are really productive, then you will need fewer workers, which means you can afford to pay more. In the food service industry the transition from a great number of unskilled low paid employees to a few high paid skilled workers will not be easy, but it can be done.

Comparisons

Once you start making and checking productivity figures on your operation, it will be possible to compare your efficiency with that of other similar places. Chains have an advantage in having a number of very similar places all doing the same thing. This makes it easy to check one against another to see which is doing the best job. Years ago, a specialty fast food operation in New York City with quite a few units received a daily sales-per-man-hour check on each place, which was posted at the main office. It was easy to see which units were productive, and which were having troubles and needed checking and more supervision. If you and I have similar operations with the same menu and sales, and you are producing $8 per man hour sales and I am only producing $6 per man hour, then I am not running my operation

at its full potential. This is a very simple way to tell quickly just how well management is performing. If you are not in a chain, then you can compare your operation with someone who has a similar facility and find out how well you are doing.

Productivity figures are valuable not only for measuring your efficiency against the competition, but also to check against past weeks or other periods of time to see if you are making any improvement or getting worse. If your sales per man hour for this week are $12/hour and were $15/hour last week or for the same week a year ago, then this is a clear signal that something is wrong. If you decide to remodel to improve efficiency and reduce operating costs, or decide to spend more time and effort in recruiting, hiring, and training to get a more productive crew, you can actually measure the results of your efforts and expenditures with the very same sales per man hour figures. If after all that remodeling and adding of new labor-saving equipment your weekly sales per man hour are the same or lower, then you have either spent a lot of money for nothing, or someone isn't working the new layout as it was meant to be worked. All of the figures you keep have a purpose if they are studied. Their main function is to serve as warning signals to you that something is starting to go wrong, giving you the chance to correct it *now*, before there is serious trouble. It is much easier to make small corrections and changes than the major changes needed when the place is really in trouble.

New Systems and Formats

Sales per man hour figures can be the best indicators of the need to make some changes in your operation. If your sales per man hour figures stay low or keep decreasing each week, despite minor changes you make in the physical plant, crew, or menus, it may be that you are in need of some major changes. In any food service operation it is always best to make as many minor, less costly improvements as possible first, to see if the facility can't be improved. In many cases, these minor changes will do the job and improve the productivity figures. However, after all of these small changes have been made and there is still no improvement, then it is time to make some real studies and come up with major changes. If the place is old, it is probably due for a face lift, changes in layout, some new equipment, new features like a bar and lounge, buffet, or salad bar, to create a new image and stimulate sales. When you have an old place it is important to remember that when it was designed and opened, it was set up with the best equipment and layout available at that time, but we have come a long way in design and equipment in recent years. Also, the restaurant was designed and set up to suit the tastes of customers years ago, but their tastes and habits have changed over the years. Even the employees back then were different from the young inexperienced people we must now work with. We do have answers today to most of these problems, and you can find them, but if you are not aware that something is wrong with your establishment, then there is little chance that you will do something to correct the faults. Keep good records and figures on your operation; check them closely each week; as soon as you detect any changes, take action right away. It is so much easier to make a minor adjustment each week than to sit by week after week doing nothing, and wake up one day to find that you have gone broke. Or if you want to trust to luck only, then take your money to the races or gambling casinos rather than open a food service establishment: your odds might be as good!

Management

As the chains grow larger and do a greater percentage of the total food service business, and "mom-pop" operations decrease, more emphasis must be placed on hired management. When the chains first started, many thought that high quality unit management would not be needed once the main office standardized the whole operation. Many still feel today that they can establish a standard format and then build hundreds of units employing weak, inexperienced unit management. Throw in several experienced supervisors and your troubles are over. The rapid proliferation of chains has changed the picture. Now that there is so much competition—business is not automatically there—you must have better unit management to meet the competition. Three years ago I moved from a small town (population 15,000) that had one national chain restaurant. At last count there were seven national chains located there—someone is going to get hurt very badly. The standard format and system will not be enough, there will be fierce competition, and the best management will win in the long run.

How do you measure the efficiency of hired unit managers? One of the best ways is with the same sales per man hour figure sent in each week. Sales figures alone are not enough because a manager can generate high sales and still lose money. Profits do not always reflect the true picture, because a manager can produce quick profits in any operation by cutting payroll, food quality, portions, etc., to make a good showing for a short period of time. That sales per man hour figure will tell you if hired management is really operating the facility and controlling the employees to get maximum productivity and efficiency. A word of advice for would-be investors and promoters in the food service industry—the food service business is not as easy as it seems. If you don't have good, experienced on-premise management, try some other line of endeavor.

The food service business is not difficult once you understand and learn the fundamentals, but many fail because they think it is very easy to make a lot of money in a very short time. In talking with people it would be very hard to find anyone who ever lost money at the race track; everyone is a winner, but I often wonder why there are all those tickets on the ground after the races are over. Many people *have* made a lot money in the food service industry, but many more have lost money. You rarely hear about these people because feature articles are not written about the failures, only about the winners.

Productivity figures might be new to you. You may never have kept them for your own operation, but it will be worth the effort to try them for a while and see just how you compare with the others.

INCREASING PRODUCTIVITY

Both sales and productivity play a major role in profits. We'll start with productivity and study the ways to increase this first. As long as it was possible to just raise prices to send sales and profits up, there was little need to work on productivity. Now that the easy way out may be coming to an end, increasing productivity and efficiency will again become important. There are some very basic rules we might want to consider:

Basic Rules for Increasing Profits
Increase what you are taking in
Decrease what you are spending or putting out

Basic Rules for Increasing Productivity
Increase sales using the same man hours
Decrease man hours while maintaining same sales

A simple explanation of the ideal approach is the use of fewer, more efficient employees who could produce more sales. Much of our thinking has been the reverse of this: using more and more inexperienced cheap help. Using the cheap help in quantity seems like the easy solution to the problem, but if we consider the increasing wage costs in our evaluation, we can see that this theory is not working too well.

Determine Your Productivity

The first step in solving any problem is to admit that the problem exists, and to determine the extent of the difficulty. Perhaps you have never figured your productivity or thought there was any reason to waste time doing so. In the previous section, specific methods were outlined on how to figure your productivity. Once you have these figures, compare them with others in the industry. Your accountant can get you figures, or local and national trade associations can provide figures for comparison. Another possibility is to compare your present productivity with that of your operation a year ago or a month ago. If your sales are slipping, wage costs going up and profits down, it is a sign that your productivity is not at its maximum. The important thing at this point is to recognize the problem and resolve to do something about it. If conditions are just starting to get worse, then the corrective steps will not be as difficult. However, if you have waited too long, then more action will be needed to get back on course.

Program to Increase Your Productivity

Now that you are determined to increase that low productivity, set up a program that you can follow. More than likely you pay wages weekly, so you can start with a weekly sales per man hour figure which can be expressed in dollars or meals. Let's assume the following weekly figures for your operation:

$7,000 total sales for week (from register readings)
$2,030 total dollar payroll (from weekly payroll sheet)
   580 total weekly man hours (from payroll sheet)

Your average hourly wage rate is $3.50 ($2,030 divided by 580 = $3.50),

29% is the percentage wage cost for the week ($2,030 divided by $7,000 = 29%), and $12.07 per man hour is your productivity figure for the week ($7,000 divided by 580 hours = $12.07/hour).

The above calculations for the week will take only a few minutes. You will have your total weekly sales in the sales book or journal taken from daily register readings. You also have the weekly payroll sheet that will give you the dollar payroll and the number of total man hours. You can buy a small notebook and record each week's figures and calculations.

Looking at the figures above we see the net results of the week are a 29 percent payroll and a $12.07 per man hour productivity figure. However, if your projected budget for payroll calls for a 26 percent payroll at this time of year, you are 3 percent too high. You don't need to wait three to six weeks for the profit and loss statement to come out and tell you the wage cost is too high. You can start to work immediately to reduce this figure; perhaps you can get it down to 26 percent by the end of the month. Looking at the chart on page 11, "Sales per Man Hour Needed to Produce Certain Wage Percent of Sales," we see that for the 26 percent wage cost you want, you need $13.46 per man hour sales. More than likely you won't be able to drop the wage cost a full 3 percent the next week, but let's say you shoot for dropping it 1½ percent to 27½ percent. If you have the same total sales of $7,000, this means reducing the dollar payroll to $1,925 ($105 reduction) or a reduction of 30 man hours when you make up next week's employee work schedule. The best way to effect this payroll trimming would be to increase sales to $7,200, then you could have a payroll of $1,980 (to give 27½ percent) which would mean only a $50 reduction in payroll—a cutting of only 14 man hours. This simple example shows how easily you can use your weekly productivity and sales figures to keep profits in line and measure your progress. If each week you compare the figures with past weeks' and with figures from similar operations, you will be well on the way to increasing productivity.

STEPS FOR INCREASING PRODUCTIVITY

In addition to setting up the system for making minor corrections each week and finding out how close or far you are from your goals, it would be wise to start on a much larger and more far-reaching program for increasing productivity. Some of the steps taken may be immediately successful, while others might take much longer to produce results. The process is similar to rebuilding a last-place baseball or football team. It takes time to find and train winning players; it is not something that can be done in a short time. Employees, including management, are one of the main ingredients for high productivity. Our customers may complain about service more than anything else, but if a poll were taken of owners and managers, help (employees) would be the number one complaint. "Just can't get good help and once we get them, we can't keep them" could be management's theme song. Two things stand out when we analyze this problem. The first thing is the food service industry's position as the biggest single employer of teenagers. This means we are starting out with a large number of young, inexperienced, and unskilled employees. Second, many reports and surveys indicate that our industry cannot afford to pay the minimum wage. We are constantly fighting to get exemption from paying this minimum at a time when other industries are paying higher and higher starting salaries and wages. It is obvious that our difficulties with employees will not be solved overnight, but we must start to turn this picture around.

Recruiting

If you want to end up with better employees, it makes sense to start out with better employees. If you are looking for a cook and rely only on a small sign in the window—"Cook Wanted"—you can be sure that you won't have many applicants to choose from. In my many years of experience, the big problem in hiring new employees has been that we did not attract enough applicants to afford a good selection. Perhaps a very small ad was placed in the newspaper the day the cook quit. Many times if we got one or two responses to the ad we were lucky. As the days wore on and we got more and more desperate, it became necessary to hire the first person we could find, or quickly put one of the dishwashers into the cooking job, hoping we could then find a dishwasher. It was a case of plugging the biggest hole first by any means possible. Gradually we slipped into operating from crisis to crisis. Rather than planning ahead for the emergencies that happen in an industry with such a high employee turnover, we were always in a sweat. Like professional sports teams, many large companies constantly recruit new people. This is just as much of a year-round job as running the operation. At least we can set up some possible sources for our future employees, establish some contacts, and know

the best place to advertise to get the people needed when the time comes. If someone comes in looking for a job and it just so happens you don't need anyone on that particular day, don't just say, "Sorry, we don't need anyone today" and let it go at that. If the applicant looks promising, take the time to talk with him/her, get the name, address, and phone number and assure him or her that you will keep the information on file. In short, build a file of people you can call on the next time you need a new employee. Take the time to call on local high schools and junior colleges and learn how you can reach these students for employment in the future. Find out the best way to reach women entering the job market (women now comprise almost 50 percent of our total work force), senior citizens, and newcomers in your community so you will have a good file and source when new employees are needed. Talk with your present employees and have them be on the lookout for good future employees. Know the people in charge of your local employment agencies so that they can help when needed. If you have a good busy operation that has fine working conditions and can match or beat the others in salaries, wages, and tips, make sure this information gets around. Before we can build a good work force, we must start with the best applicants possible. The more people you have on file and the more that show up for interviews, the better selection you can make to fill that opening. If only one person shows up for the job, you really don't have much choice. More than likely you will be soon looking to fill the same job again. This is one of the main reasons for high employee turnover.

Hiring

Once you have attracted the applicants, then comes the important task of interviewing and hiring. In most cases not enough time is given to interviewing and hiring in our industry. Many interviews are hurried because the manager or owner is busy and is constantly interrupted by phone calls or by problems needing his or her attention. This means that the management does not find out much about the applicant, and the applicant learns less about the job and the company he or she is about to work for. With this sketchy introduction it is little wonder if the wrong people are hired, or if new employees soon find out that the job is not for them. Many managers have told me that they just don't have the time to interview properly and must rely on instinct to judge whether the applicant is right for the job. What a way to run a business! This is about the only opportunity you will have to get pertinent information on the prospective employee; take the time to conduct a good interview.

First of all the applicant should fill out the application form in detail. You should have looked over this application before beginning the interview to make notes and think of additional questions. While you are using the interview to get important information from the applicant, you should also be presenting all information concerning the job: job description, company benefits, conditions, and terms so that the applicant will have a clear understanding of the duties and responsibilities. This is the moment for both parties to present information and learn as much as they can so there will be no misunderstandings in the future. It is important to realize that while you are choosing an employee the applicant is also selecting a job and future employer. This is the time to bring out all good features and any unfavorable things that may exist.

Once the applicant has presented all the information required and has received full details about the job, then references and other information given need to be checked. Many say they do not have the time to do this or, that if they take the time, the applicant will not wait and will take another job. Because more and more companies are checking out this information before hiring, applicants know they will not be hired immediately. If you want a charge card you must fill out the application and wait until your credit has been checked. If the job is not important enough to require a little investigation before hiring, or the applicant is not willing to wait a few days before being accepted, then the whole transaction cannot be too worthwhile. I would be a little suspicious of a job if I walked in and the employer quickly said "You're hired, start immediately!" We are also assuming that you have improved your recruiting so that there will be more than one applicant to interview and you will be wanting to see them all before making a choice. Once again, if I found out that I was the only applicant for a job, I would wonder what was wrong with the job or the company. Screen all applicants, check their references carefully, and you will have better employees to start with. Take as much time as possible to make sure the applicant is the right person for the job. When you give the applicant full information about the job and the company, you are making it easier for him/her to decide if this job is worth a trial. Continual recruiting, hiring, and training is much more expensive and time consuming than making a little more effort at the initial interview.

Salaries and Wages

For many in our industry salaries and wages are difficult subjects. Some even try to avoid them. However in your effort to raise productivity and get good employees, the amount of money you pay is an important factor. Although some go so far as to say that they can get and keep employees without paying going rates, in most instances the employee knows what others are making. Perhaps you might get away with paying less for a short time, but sooner or later the problem must be faced. If your operation cannot afford to pay going rates or compete on the job market, then you must be resigned to taking whatever employees you can get, if and when you can find any. More than likely they will be young and inexperienced, or transients constantly going from one job to another. When you pay under the market, many of the employees you get will be taking the job only for a short time to supplement income or as a stopgap until they can find a better job. In any event, the beginning employees you'll get under these circumstances are not ones who will turn into highly productive, skilled employees later on. Will you save money by paying less and hiring these young, unskilled, and uninterested employees? Evidently many in our industry think the answer is yes. We continue to use many people like this, and continue to have a very high employee turnover. If the hourly dollar-and-cent wage were the only cost, then I might agree to paying as little as possible. But when I look at the costs for laundry, employees' meals, taxes, insurance, breakage, pilferage, hiring, training, and fringe benefits that must be added to that "dollar and cents per hour," then my vote goes for having fewer, but better trained, productive employees who are paid a little more per hour! If you have a food service operation with 100 employees and have a 200 percent turnover (this is not a high turnover in this industry), you are hiring 200 people a year. This means that about every two days you have a new employee who must be indoctrinated and trained. This alone is enough to ruin your productivity figures for the year. Many will say that pay and salary are not the most important factors, but if you are paying below scale then the dollar sign takes on new meaning. This idea is well illustrated by an article in *Nation's Restaurant News* (October 1, 1979):

Maine Restaurant Shows Profit in Its First Year

PORTLAND, Me.— When the owners of the Baker's Table, a restaurant in a converted 177-year-old warehouse, completed their first year in business they were in the black with a net of $50,000 on sales of $500,000.

They concluded it was a good year. Despite a relatively high level of food and labor costs, about 40% each, they expect to change little.

"Many restaurants open here and in their first year they struggle. We didn't," said Ken Thomas, one of four owners.

"Our formula is good."

He said turnover is nearly nonexistent among his 31 employees. "Instead of a pat on the back we give them money and we provide insurance. Most of our employees are college graduates. We don't pick a bum on the street and employ him. We pick someone who is qualified to do the job, people who want to stay.

"We'd rather do this instead of making a killing and then having our chefs throw knives at each other," said Thomas, an artist, designer and contractor.

A very simple labor policy is set forth in this article: "Give them money." "We pick someone who is qualified to do the job, *people who want to stay.*" There is little need for a labor relations expert here with a simple successful formula like this.

Training

The next important step in building a productive work force is to start and maintain a good training program for all new employees. One of the food service industry's biggest weaknesses is the lack of training and indoctrination. Employees are hired and put on jobs with no training or assistance at all. The total orientation session might consist of telling the new employee, "Watch what Joe is doing," or "If you have any questions, ask Mary!" The sad part about this is that Joe and Mary had the same training program, so it is doubtful whether they know what they are doing.

Many years ago we filmed (with a hidden camera) a busy kitchen in action, and then studied the film to point up the need for better training and job efficiency. People who watched this film could not believe what employees were doing to get the food out, and it was quickly decided that better training would be worthwhile. The great majority of food service operations cannot afford training centers, or staff paid to concentrate on training only. Most of our training is "on the job." It's conducted by management or key personnel. The important thing is to make sure that management and the key employees know what they are doing and can give the right instructions to the new employees. Management must know the right and most efficient way to do each job; you cannot leave it up to the employees (especially the new ones) to figure out. People can do things the hard way for years until someone steps forward and shows them a simpler and more efficient way. Spend several hours sometime watching your crew in action; notice the great amount of effort, wasted motions, and extra steps and you will soon come up with many ideas to improve productivity. In many cases you don't need to be a "time and motion" expert to figure out easier and faster ways to do things. After all, this is exactly what the productivity and efficiency experts do. They get paid good money for doing something that you could do with a little time and effort.

One morning I watched a woman working in a school lunch kitchen whose particular job it was to get canned peach halves and dish them up. She started by making about six trips to the storeroom bringing back several cans in her apron and putting them on a table. Once this was accomplished, she had to carry two cans at a time to another table where the can opener was, open each can, and carry them back. Then she dumped each can into a mixing bowl on a dolly. The empty cans were then taken to the trash can (another three or four trips). The next step was to dish up peach halves into small dishes and put them on trays. As each tray was finished, it was carried by itself across the kitchen to the reach-in refrigerator. When this was done it was necessary to take the mixing bowl to the dish room so it could be washed. Needless to say, this procedure took a long time and a lot of walking. How could this have been done more easily? Take a utility truck and go to the storeroom and bring out the two or three cases of canned peaches needed in one trip. Cut off the tops of the cases and then open the six cans with an electric can opener, which can be moved around the kitchen. You can open the cans without taking them from the case. Serve the peaches directly from the cans into the dishes, put the trays of dished up peaches into another mobile rack that can be wheeled over to the refrigerator in one trip. Take the empty cartons and cans in one trip to the trash area, and the job is done. The kitchen I was analyzing had seven employees all working very hard to do very simple tasks which could have been done by three people who had some training and instructions on how to do the various jobs. You can't be productive if you are constantly walking or doing unnecessary work.

Turnover

Figures given for labor turnover in the food service industry are very high; they range from 100 to 300 percent. We have already noted many reasons for this, but it is very obvious that not only is this high turnover costly, but it is a big factor in causing the low productivity in food service. When you have a constant parade of employees coming and going it is extremely unlikely that they will be highly productive. In some instances the new employees do not stay long enough to get minimum job orientation, let alone adequate training. One large chain a few years ago had an average stay of 28 days for its servers! Very few food service operations have a complete file on their employees or could tell you how many employees were hired in the past year, or how many were fired or quit. Exit interviews help determine why employees quit. This is a good idea to keep in mind. You may find a definite pattern that will show you why so many are leaving, and what you should do to stop the exodus. Before deciding that this is just another one of those records and figures you don't need, acknowledge that high turnover is a very real, high-cost item in your operation. It isn't listed on your profit and loss statement as "turnover," but it will make itself known in higher wage costs and lower profits. If you are at all interested in higher profits, lower wage costs, and higher employee productivity, then reduce your employee turnover as much as possible.

Job Descriptions

One very basic approach to preventing personnel problems and increasing productivity is making up and using job descriptions. My first encounter with job descriptions came back in the thirties, when an expert came to our company to set up better labor relations. We in operations were asked to make up written job descriptions for all of the people in the organization including ourselves. What a silly waste of time, we thought. Of course we all knew what was involved in each job or position—or did we? When the time came to actually put on paper the duties of a "busperson," "short order cook," or "waiter/waitress" it became apparent that we in management did not know what was required of the people we were directing. This in turn meant that they did not know what was expected of them. Just the act of writing those descriptions taught us more about our employees and their jobs than we could have learned from years of watching them. It suddenly dawned on us that it was little wonder that most of our employees were failing to do their jobs well. Not only did *we* not know what the job entailed, but *they* had never really been instructed in their duties and responsibilities. It was much like trying to reach a solution without knowing what the problem was.

One other side effect of writing these job descriptions was the discovery that when all of the duties and responsibilities of the unit managers were finally put down on paper, the list was so long and complicated that it would have taken two people working 24 hours a day to really accomplish them. Needless to say, many beneficial changes resulted from our first encounter with job descriptions, and I am sure that putting these things down on paper would surprise many in the industry who have never done this before.

Degree of Difficulty

One stumbling block in increasing employee productivity today is the increasing degree of job difficulty in the food service industry. In the early days we had a great number of employees each confined to a limited area and duties. Kitchens were huge and were divided into separate departments, each staffed with employees assigned to specialized jobs: broil, fry, sauté, roast, vegetable preparation, salads, desserts, fish, butcher, pastries, beverages, etc. Having a great number of specialized employees with a very low turnover meant labor problems were practically nonexistent. This climate, in which the food service industry started and grew, explains the reluctance of many to welcome changes or make much effort to improve productivity and efficiency. Just recently we have begun to see the food service industry take advantage of innovations such as energy-saving equipment and systems. The equipment we are seeing, such as heat recovery systems, is not new; it has been around for years, but our industry has been very slow to change the status quo and accept new ideas.

The fast food industry is fortunate in offering jobs with a low degree of difficulty. Fast food operations have very limited menus, little or no food preparation, and as much automated equipment as possible. Their jobs are

broken down so that each employee has limited duties and responsibilities. This makes it possible for the fast food industry to use young and unskilled people and train them very quickly so that they can be productive in a matter of days or even hours. As food service operations change more to full menus, heavy preparation, and service, the degree of difficulty increases. In addition to the increase in the degree of difficulty, we are faced with the problem of being able to afford fewer employees because wage rates are higher, so that the employees must assume more duties and responsibilities, or wear "many hats." This increases the problems of finding and training multi-talented help, and of course reduces productivity. At a time when it is difficult to find even untrained people to perform the simplest tasks, it is almost impossible to find people with many skills who are highly productive and willing to work for low wage rates.

Food Preparation

It has taken many years, but the food service industry is finally deciding that its business is primarily "serving" and not "preparing"! Work really started on frozen and convenience foods back in the forties, but acceptance has been very slow. One of the best ways to quickly increase productivity, sales, and profits is to cut food preparation to a minimum. The amount of preparation, or back of the house work, will depend on the check average and the number of people to be fed. If you have a very high check average with few people to feed, then you can afford more "from scratch" food preparation. As you come down the ladder in check averages, but increase the numbers to be fed (as you would in a fast food operation), your attention must shift from preparation to service. Many of the fast food operations now do little or no preparation and direct efforts to service. This explains their high per-unit gross sales and productivity despite limited, low priced menus. McDonald's at one time bought potatoes in the bag and featured the peeling, cutting, and frying of fresh potatoes, but has now dropped this practice in favor of buying frozen, blanched french fried potatoes. We could get into arguments about quality and taste of convenience foods as opposed to foods prepared from scratch that would fill several books, but the bottom line is still productivity, sales, and profits. The more you concentrate on selling and serving, and cut down on "nonproductive preparation," the better chance you will have to build volume, sales, and profits. The selection of convenience foods is so great today that restaurant operators can easily find most of the foods they serve already prepared. Those who argue about quality should take into account that the odds for foods being prepared correctly from scratch today by the great number of unskilled employees are not too good. Over the years I have been served a lot of poor "from scratch" foods!

Management

The need for competent leadership has never been greater in the food service industry. This applies not only to the top brass, but down through middle management to unit management. Because of the huge growth in chains, we are seeing more and more hired rather than owner management. This adds to the difficulty, because hired management does not have the same zeal and dedication. In addition, we are facing a period in which top management is becoming more interested in finances and speculation than food service. Much effort is directed to opening a great number of units fast to make a big splash, and of course a fast buck. Many are setting up a format and design and stamping them out with the speed of new cars on an assembly line. They believe there is no problem in finding unit management or employees, because the system has been worked out to perfection by the top brass.

A lot of this modern theory is starting to come apart at the seams. No matter how good your main office or top executives, if you don't have competent unit management, forget it! It's like hiring the best coach available and giving him poor players; the team won't win many games. Given a choice, I would prefer strong unit management and weak middle and top management. One of the major chains recently ran into major financial trouble because of weak, overworked unit management. The turnover of their unit managers was 75 percent (out of every 100 managers they were losing 75), making the profitable management of their many food service operations, spread out over the country, very difficult. The chain had also decided to stay open 24 hours a day, adding more problems to an already tough situation. With all the problems today of competition, inflation, energy, and government regulations, you had better find the best management possible if you want to stay in business. This means unit or on-premise management. You can have the sharpest top executives in the world, but if you don't have strong management on the job directing the operations every day, your chances for success will be slim. It is hard to keep good employees if you don't have strong unit managers. Employees soon learn how good their manager is and won't stay long if he/she is weak. Many of the problems in the food service industry today can be traced directly to poor management. If the facility doesn't have knowledgeable management present to train and direct inexperienced employees, there is just no way to get any kind of high employee productivity. If no one in the operation knows what to do, success is very doubtful.

Tension and Friction

In the article reprinted previously "Maine Restaurant Shows Profit in Its First Year," one quote is particularly interesting: "We rather do this than making a killing and then having our chefs throw knives at each other." Several times in my career in food service I have actually seen knives thrown—this is not a remote possibility. Unless you have actually run a very busy food service operation, you may not realize how much tension, friction, and pressure there is on the employees. It is a difficult business requiring much physical exertion; working conditions are not the best. Many kitchens are scenes of noise, confusion, shouting, heat, and short tempers. The cooks are not too sympathetic to the waiters/waitresses; because servers' incomes depend largely on tips, they constantly put pressure on cooks to get their orders out fast so that customers will be happy, and management is always under pressure from all sides—customers, employees, owners, stockholders, government agencies, etc. It is little wonder that during rush periods many food service operations are like battlefields.

Does this pressure and confusion have an adverse effect on productivity? Most certainly, because no one can work smoothly and efficiently under these conditions. We know that many food service employees leave very soon after starting on the job. Many years ago people in our industry boasted about their ability to take punishment; to "make the grade" a food service employee had to be able to tolerate long hours, great pressure, and hard physical exertion. Some other industries also required quite a bit of effort, but today this hard work has been eliminated from jobs in most industries. Employees are not willing to suffer this kind of punishment day after day, especially for below-average wages. Is this pressure and physical exertion necessary in food service today? Again, absolutely not! Knowledgeable management using modern layouts, and new equipment, techniques, and systems can eliminate most of the tension and friction in any food service operation. What a pleasure it is to visit the kitchen of a well-run food facility during a busy period and note the smoothness and precision of the operation. Not only are noise and shouting missing, but very few words will be spoken while placing and picking up orders from the kitchen. It's just the other side of that old slogan, "When in doubt, run about and shout!"

Working Conditions

The effect of working conditions on productivity is another of those factors so hard to measure in any industry. You just can't come up with a dollar figure and say, "Look, here's how much you are losing by having poor working conditions for your employees." We do know that poor conditions affect employee morale and lower productivity. Many of the strikes called by unions are to get better and safer working conditions for the members. Many food service operations lack things like lockers, space for dressing, employee dining areas, areas for taking a break, employee toilets, proper ventilation in working areas, and good tools and equipment to do the job. Many of these may seem trivial, and not important to employees, but repeated exit interviews show that as many people quit because of the little things as do over pay. If our industry were known for its high wage scale, perhaps we could get away with poor working conditions, but we are not.

In times of recession, when jobs are hard to get, it is hard to see the need to improve working conditions because employees will put up with anything just to be working. When inflation boom times come, the owners say they cannot afford these frills and fringe benefits. Many times complete provisions are planned for the employees, but when the cost estimates come in for building and equipment, reductions are made. Employee facilities are the first to be cut because they are seen as not absolutely necessary. It is high time for many to realize that the days of "Tote that barge, lift that bale" are over. If we expect to attract and keep better employees, the industry had better improve working conditions. If you have ever had your watch or wallet stolen because no locker was provided for safekeeping of your valuables while you worked, you can appreciate the fact that these are not little things.

Plan Layout and Equipment

Proper layout and equipment can increase productivity. Our industry is not completely sold on this premise, but nevertheless, it is true. We know that our employees spend too much time walking and wasting effort in other ways. This in itself can cut productivity in any industry. Assembly-line techniques were developed many years ago to combat just this sort of waste. Instead of having workers running back and forth, work was brought directly to the employees who could then stand still and really produce. Visit the large food processing plants and you will see workers seated at conveyor belts. This way they can work efficiently, using only their hands, while the work goes by on the belt. Contrast this with the average food service facility where the employees are running around like people trying out for the Olympics. Proper layout would place the equipment where it is needed and eliminate a lot of this wasted effort.

Once you have the best possible layout, giving you a good work and product flow, then concentrate on selecting equipment that will save man hours. Get as much automatic or semi-automatic equipment as possible to help all those inexperienced employees in their jobs. Look into the many small pieces of miscellaneous equipment now available that can save time and effort. For example, if you sell a lot of seafood and iced tea, and need lemon wedges, instead of having someone cut each wedge by hand, get one of those sectioning machines and do the job in a fifth of the time. Think of the lowly can opener; no matter how big the kitchen, most places will only have one opener, fixed in one place, so that all cans must be carried to this spot. Is there any law against having two openers and saving most of that wasted time and motion?

Have enough equipment to do the job. One of the most time-consuming aspects of work in many food service operations is finding the equipment when and where needed. This applies particularly to service ware, dishes, cups, glasses, flatware, small utensils, and pans. Many of these items are expensive, so people are reluctant to put them into circulation, theorizing that the less you put in service, the less you will lose or break. It is very difficult to serve food well and fast when you can't find something to serve it in or on! Just to get the record straight, if you are short of service equipment *in service* (many have plenty of serving equipment that is in some storeroom collecting dust) you will have more breakage and much slower service.

Another serious problem with equipment today is keeping it operating and in repair. Repair and maintenance are getting more costly. In some cases it's even hard to get them done. If major pieces of equipment like ice machines and dish machines are not working, you can have serious trouble. Major pieces of equipment are costly; it would pay to look into preventive mainte-

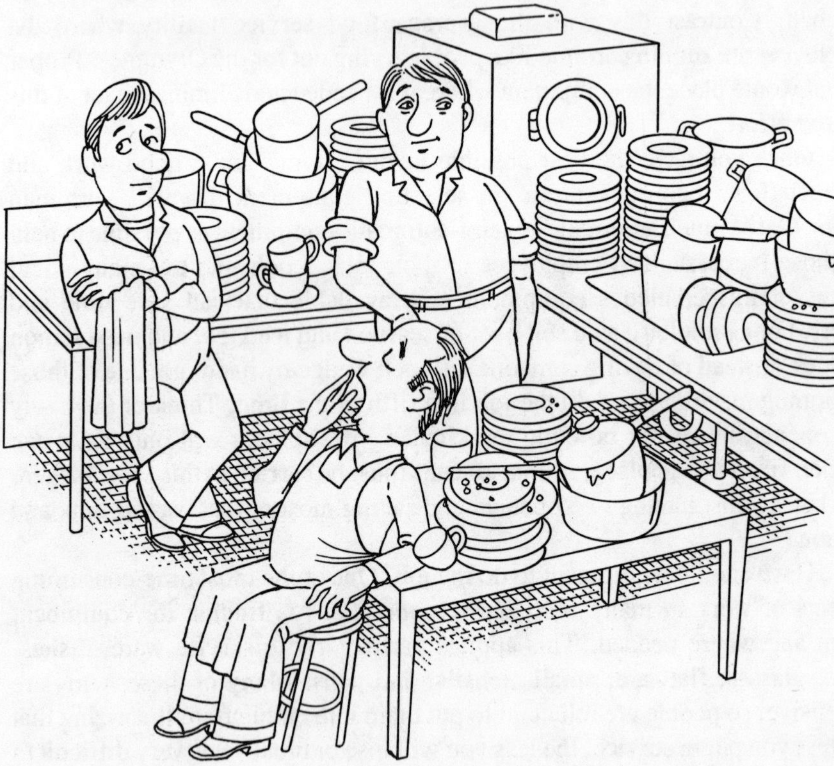

nance programs for many of them. If your walk-in freezer or refrigerator go out for any length of time, the losses can be huge. Good labor-saving equipment won't help increase productivity if it is inoperative.

Last on the list of proper selection and use of equipment is the instruction of employees in its proper use. We not only have a serious problem of a very high injury rate in our industry, but no piece of equipment can be of use if people don't know how to use it. Most dishwashers run at 35 percent of their capacity because employees have not been shown how to sort, rack, feed, and unload ware to cut running time to a minimum. Slicing machines are doing a bad job of cutting because few know how to work the blade sharpeners; in one kitchen the staff did not even know the slicer had a sharpener. We now have small tomato slicers that will slice a tomato perfectly into even slices in one second. I have seen kitchens with these machines back on a shelf because one of the blades broke and new blades were never ordered. We have the equipment to cut your labor and increase productivity, but in addition to buying it, someone must take the time to learn how it works and instruct others.

Employees' Performance

The measure of your productivity will depend to a great degree on how well each employee performs his/her job. Getting what you paid for is an important part of what we define as *control*. This means not only goods, but services as well. Services include the services of architects, attorneys, or designers, and it certainly means the services of your employees. You are paying them for a service (or making it possible for them to earn tips), and depending on how well they perform, you could get your money's worth or be shortchanged. The higher the salaries and wages, the more you should expect in return.

It is unreasonable to expect 100 percent cooperation from all employees at all times, but if you have even a few (especially in key positions) who are not contributing their share, then the productivity of the entire operation will suffer. Not only are these non-producers hurting the boss, they are increasing the load for employees who are trying to do a good job. Unfortunately we do not have a scale or device for measuring performance, but there are some things that can be done. For employees in serving and selling we can tabulate individual sales. If one server writes only 50 percent as much in checks as others, we have reason to believe that he/she is not producing and should be helped or replaced. Hired management performance can be measured by the amount of sales and profits produced, as well as the productivity figures of sales per man hour or sales per employee per year. If management is really close to the operation in training, actually supervising, and providing the right kind of leadership, it will know from visual contact which employees are or are not producing. This is one reason why it is so important for management to be out on the firing line during at least the start of each busy period, rather than back in the office or away from the operation. We do have some fine systems today for the control of food service operations, but nothing beats being right on the job to see what is happening. Very few customers take the time to actually make a complaint to management; they just mumble to themselves and never come back.

Maintain Communication

Many problems between workers and their bosses are the result of a lack of communication. The good boss or leader is the one who stays in complete touch with his/her fellow workers at all times. When management starts to drift away from the day-to-day or hour-to-hour operation and has less and less contact with the employees, then the troubles start. The rank and file employees are no longer getting the training and direction they need to perform their jobs well. Cooperation between the various departments and employees starts to break down, and internal trouble and dissension result. The breakdown in communication also means management is not getting accurate information on how the business is really going. Perhaps you have seen places that just seem to be going downhill like this. This is the one big problem in franchising. It is easy to find people to invest and buy franchises. Outside investors think the food service business is easy, and that there is a fortune to be made. However, few franchisees realize the amount of work and long hours needed to properly supervise a food service facility. They start out strong, but soon weaken and turn the place over to a young inexperienced manager. Soon the operation begins to go downhill. The franchisee has lost communication with his/her manager and eventually will lose the franchise itself.

Scheduling

The necessity of making up employee work schedules is another of those old basic rules like "keep hot foods hot, and cold foods cold" that everyone

Increasing Productivity and Sales

knows but forgets to do. Most of the failures in business can be traced to someone not doing the very simple and obvious things needed for success. Many operators do not spend the time necessary on careful scheduling of employees each week. Much scheduling is accomplished verbally. Sometimes employees are simply told to follow the previous week's days and hours. If you want to improve productivity and eliminate those wasted man hours, it will pay to make up a written schedule of hours and days each week for your employees. In this way, you can study all of the sales figures (weekly, daily, and hourly) and adjust your schedule to give you the best coverage with the minimum number of hours. Remember that one formula for productivity is sales (or meals) divided by man hours, so if you plan carefully each week and reduce those man hours, your productivity will be higher. Not only must you cut wasted man hours during slow periods, but you must make sure there is enough help to fully cover the busy times to produce maximum sales. If you *cut man hours* and *increase sales* at the same time, your productivity will really rise.

The next time you go into a restaurant and wait 45 minutes in line, and then sit at the table for a long time waiting for service, you can be fairly certain that someone has not scheduled enough help to take care of the peak periods. Considering that the average restaurant is busy only 30 percent of the time, it is imperative to serve as many people as possible during those rush periods.

Maximizing Busy Periods

In a short time, your sales figures will tell you exactly when the rushes hit and how severe they are. The better you are set up and prepared for these busy periods, the fewer serving delays you will have, and the more customers you can serve. Have all foods ready at point of use; service stations should be completely stocked with all the items the waiters and waitresses need. Check to see that all employees are ready on station, and know exactly what to do. The worst part of the rush is right at the start when all the seats are first filled. If you have 100 seats, you will suddenly have about 75 people to serve at the same time. If you are not ready, you will be stuck right from the beginning and you will stay stuck through most of the serving period. If you are able to take care of this initial crush, the rest of the meal will consist of a few customers coming and going, a situation that is much easier to handle. It is very important that everyone and everything be ready for that initial onslaught; once you get by this, things will be easier and the service will be fast.

These sales figures will also point out your slow periods. These slow periods can be organized to maximize your employees' productivity. The more nonproductive work (work that is not directly connected to selling and serving) you can do during those slow periods, the better. Most or all of the food preparation can be done during the slow times. Many restaurants prepare food in large quantities and then freeze it to cut down on preparation time. All cleaning and set up work can be done during the off periods so that everyone is ready for the rushes. Inventories, interviews with sales representatives, ordering, receiving, and storing goods can be arranged for the slow times of the days, as can other office work, bookkeeping, and phone calls. Many places now do most of their warewashing during the slow times and concentrate on busing, sorting, and stacking during rush periods, so that more emphasis can be placed on serving and turnover. Many places do not call managers and employees to the phone during meal periods but take messages. In short, get all of the nonproductive work done during the slow times, so that you can be ready when business comes. For many the tendency is to let down and rest after the rush, but it won't be long before the next serving period comes. It will be better for all if things are ready. For best productivity, keep man hours low during the slow periods, and concentrate employees and man hours in the busy times.

Assist and Reward

Successful management today must be able to train and help employees in every way possible. The best qualification for a good manager is to be a good leader. Many years ago we could afford "bosses" because there was an ample supply of experienced cheap help to fill all jobs. If any employee did not measure up to the standards set, he or she was fired immediately and replaced. Now, with the shortage of both skilled and unskilled help in food service, management must take a different approach. First of all you are not going to quickly find those highly qualified employees who can step into a job and be productive with minimum training in a matter of hours or days. Most of the new employees you find will be young with little or no experience and only a small amount of ambition. The trick is to take these people and train them so that they can contribute to the operation in a relatively short time. If they are not helped when first starting, and they find the job too difficult, more than likely they will throw in the towel and seek employment elsewhere. If they are

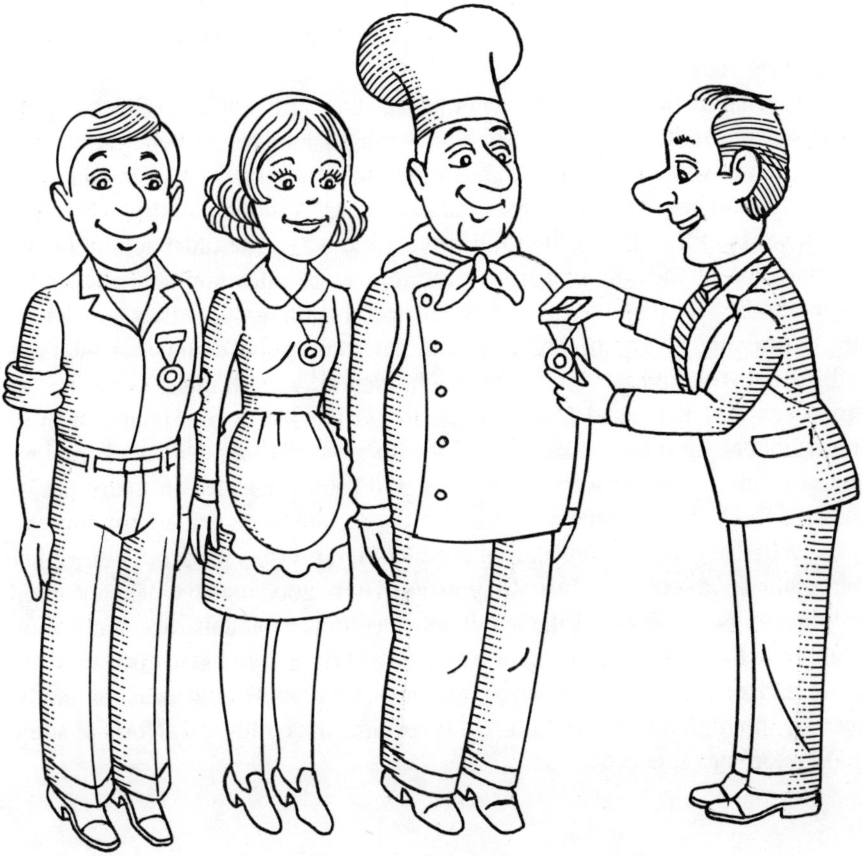

working mainly for tips, but are not taking home a sizeable amount after a very short time, they will be forced to leave and find another job where the tips are better.

Management has a big load to carry today. Many of the employees are not enthusiastic or eager to learn. Management has the job of expertly leading, directing, helping, and rewarding people in order to get results. Even monkeys learn much faster when a banana is presented to them every time they do something right!

Earlier we discussed the matter of pay. One of the basic problems in the food service industry is that our hourly wages and fringe benefits are not competitive with the labor market in general. In fact, the gap is widening between food service and many smaller industries in the country. There are two schools of thought in the food service industry. The older school favors continuance of the low or below minimum wage rates and dependence on large numbers of unskilled employees to get the job done. Others are changing—choosing to pay higher wages to get some good employees who are willing to work and who stay on the job. Naturally, with this second type of employee you will need fewer people to get the job done. Having been in management for many years, I will go with a few skilled, dedicated employees any time. Having seen the service and food presented in many places today, I think the customers would also appreciate more skilled employees.

Whether you are considering productivity, profits, service, or any other part of the food service industry, if you don't have good management and good employees on the job, all the seminars, meetings, manuals, and motivation training in the world will be of little help. We must not only give good food but good service as well to be successful. Ours is a complex business, as can be seen by the high number of failures. It requires the combined efforts of some good people to succeed.

INTERRELATION OF SALES AND PRODUCTIVITY

Before getting into the details of how to increase sales, it might be wise to investigate the close relationship between sales and productivity. Most in our industry are very familiar with sales, but there are not too many people who talk in terms of productivity or take the time to measure it.

The basic formula for determining productivity is sales (in terms of dollars, meals, or units) divided by the number of employees or man hours to get a measure of efficiency. The answer could be $14 per man hour, $20,000 per employee/per year, or six trays per minute depending on your operation and method of calculation.

Sales are not only a measure of productivity, but can be the result as well. The amount of sales enables you to calculate the degree of productivity, but at the same time the productivity you have will determine the amount of your sales. If you have an inexperienced, untrained crew working with old equipment and a poor physical layout, the odds are you will have low productivity and low sales. However, if you have a situation like many fast food operations, with high unit sales, good systems, and physical setups that fully utilize young inexperienced employees, your productivity will be high. In fact, fast food operations rank among the top of sales per employee per year, despite their low average check and inexperienced help.

These figures can highlight other unusual circumstances. It is possible to have high sales with low productivity. Not all food service operations get into trouble because of low sales. Many *do* have the sales volume, but because of poor management, bad layouts, etc. they are forced to use far more employees than the place can afford, and losses result despite the high sales. Sometimes we can find instances of high productivity with low sales. It may be difficult for some places to get or keep enough help; they are always operating with a crew that's at a minimum even for the small amount of sales. The employees they have are always pushed to the limit, which explains why they don't stay on the job too long. But while they are there they are really pushing out the food, making their productivity figures really high.

In any analysis or study, do not draw conclusions based on very short-term figures. In food service it is possible to produce some remarkable results for a short period of time that will not hold up in the long haul. When people get ready to sell restaurants they can really go out and produce some excellent operating figures for a short time, but look at the long-term profit and loss statements before buying. You can give any place a quick shot in the arm or briefly cut costs to the bone, but how long can this last?

Sales are the measure of productivity, but when sales go up it doesn't always mean your crew has suddenly become more efficient and productive. This can be seen by what has happened in the industry. The steady sharp increase in menu prices that has naturally increased sales has been interpreted by many as a sign of more customers and increased productivity and efficiency, when actually most of the sales increase has been due solely to the higher prices. We have really seen "EWO" (Easy Way Out) at work for years. As long as the public can and will pay any amount for eating out, then there is little reason to worry about the future. As a food service consultant I have noticed a change in attitudes. Before the boom times, many called in consultants to help plan less costly and more efficient facilities. As selling prices, sales, and profits continued to skyrocket, there was less need for careful, studied planning. The attitude embraced by many food service operators was, "Just get the places built and open to cash in on the big bonanza!" There are two things wrong with this type of thinking. First of all economic conditions always change; what goes up must come down, and sooner or later the gravy train will slow down or come to a halt. When that happens it is too late to think about design, layout, and systems to produce maximum sales with minimum effort and man hours. Second, we have the money to spend on research and development only during the boom times. If we don't set aside some of the profits at that time to learn more efficient methods and increase productivity, it will never be done; in times of recessions and depressions there are no extra funds to spare. When times are good and profits high, what's wrong with a little research and study to increase profits further? Then if business starts to slump, we will be ready for that too. It is difficult to think ahead and not just sit back and enjoy the fruits of the present, but this is necessary. If we had any idea of what we were doing back in the thirties when food and labor were so cheap, we could have made twice as much money as we did. This is where good seasoned management is so important. We need people who can gather facts and figures and then really use them to plan for the future.

FOOD SERVICE SALES

The second part of this manual has to do with food service sales. Anyone in business, whether it be involved with a product or service, is familiar with the term sales because this is one measure of the success of any venture. It is not the only measure—there are other considerations, such as costs and profits. Many people in business make the mistake of focusing all of their attention on certain areas only, neglecting other parts that may be just as important. Some think only of sales and forget costs and profits; others spend all of their time cutting costs to the detriment of sales and growth; most in business will say, "Never mind all of these figures on the page, just show me the bottom line." Cutting every penny possible from costs and squeezing the last dollar from the profits can hurt a business in the long run by lowering sales and stopping needed growth. For best results, management should be interested in all of the figures and try to get the best balance to achieve the needed profits and growth.

NEW EMPHASIS ON SELLING

In analyzing food service sales the first thing to consider is that our industry is in the unique role of manufacturing and selling in the same place. This means that in addition to other distractions from selling, we have the problem of spending more time, money, and effort on the preparation and cooking than the serving and selling. As operating costs go up and the need for more sales becomes urgent, more and more people in the food service industry must reach a decision. Are they in the food service and selling business or in the food manufacturing business? Many years ago there was little choice because there were no convenience or prepared foods available and everything had to be made from scratch on premise. There were some canned foods (not the quality of today's) but no frozen foods as we know them. Almost every item was bought fresh (in season), prepared, cooked, and served on premise. Fortunately we also had a large group of skilled inexpensive help so that all of this work and effort was no problem. Food was also very cheap, so pilferage and waste caused little concern. Managing these places meant most of the time was spent in the "back of the house" supervising all of the purchasing, receiving, storage, and cooking. By comparison, far less time and effort was placed on serving and selling. This part of the business sort of took care of itself. You could afford plenty of waiters/waitresses because they received no wages (tips only) and of course there was little or no advertising or promotion. Courses in food management were definitely slanted to cooking, not serving, and this attitude remains today in many schools and food service operations. The fact that poor service is still the number one customer complaint bears out the fact that many still think that this is a business of cooking, not serving and selling. In fact, other than in fast food operations, when was the last time you saw a manager in a table service operation out front working or supervising service in the dining areas?

    Many in our industry are now realizing the importance of selling and putting the money and effort out front where the customers and cash registers are located. That beautiful preparation kitchen with the full array of chefs, butchers, and bakers is fine for the awards and articles in trade magazines but means little to the customer who never sees either. The customer is only concerned about what happens in the dining area, particularly at the table. The tremendous growth of the fast food industry is evidence of the fact that when emphasis is placed on serving and selling, increased sales, growth, and profit are the result. McDonald's is a perfect example, with average unit sales of $975,000. This means they have many places doing over $1 million a year in sales. This is almost double the average sales for Howard Johnson's ($550,000 per unit per year) who have full-scale restaurants open *24 hours a day*. McDonald's spends as much on advertising as 25 of the top 100 chains each bring in in total sales! Visit any McDonald's during the rush periods and you will find the manager and all the employees out front and ready to *serve* the customers.

We are seeing many new restaurants being opened by young people. These are usually theme places where most of the effort and money is being put out front in decor and surroundings. Even the new young managers can be found in the dining rooms trying to improve service and customer relations. No one will ever settle the argument about good food versus good service, but one thing is sure today. Higher unit sales are not only a help, but are necessary in solving the many problems existing in the food service industry. If you ever get caught in the downward spiral of decreasing sales, increasing costs, more sales decreases, and higher costs, you will realize the importance of sales. The place with the high sales is also the easiest to manage, because you can afford the skilled help you need, and high sales will compensate for a multitude of errors.

MEASURING SALES

Another misconception about sales is that the only sales figure is the one that shows up on the profit and loss statement. All you have to do is take the register readings at the end of each day, add them up, and you get monthly and yearly gross sales figures. Of course you must do this for tax purposes, but what could be easier anyway? Judging from the minimal records many food service operations keep, some would not have even the total sales figures if recording them were not required by law. In arriving at answers and solutions it is always best to understand the problem. If we are to do anything about sales, then we must know more than the one yearly gross sales figure. One million dollars a year in sales would be a blessing for a place that has been doing $750,000 a year, but would mean disaster for another place that has been doing $1.5 million a year. It's much like handing someone hired to solve your operating problems a figure of $2,150 and saying, "That's my payroll," without giving any other information or details. I was called in one day to evaluate a restaurant that was about to add a new dining room. I went to the site and talked with the manager who reported sales of about $850. On my way back to talk with the owner I thought: $850/day; $5,000/week; $250,000/year; there might be enough here to pay off the new addition. When the owner informed me that the $850 was the *weekly* sales, the picture changed completely. With sales this low, what was needed was a new restaurant in another location.

Total Yearly Sales

Yearly sales provide a good figure for comparisons because this is usually the figure reported in financial statements or in the surveys made on various chains and companies. This is also the figure most important to stockbrokers and their clients.

Monthly or Period Sales

Most operations use calendar months, but some prefer the 13 (four-week) period system for their accounting and for their profit and loss statements. In most food service operations the inventories are taken once a month, when costs such as food and beverage are figured. The 13-period accounting method is good because it gives equal periods having the same number of weekends, making it easy to compare them to previous years.

Weekly Sales

The weekly sales figures are becoming more important in the control of food service operations that want to detect and remedy weaknesses as fast as possible to keep on a good sound financial course. The results of the monthly profit and loss statement can come too late to help. By the time the inventories are taken, priced, extended, and totaled, and the statement is ready it will be the 10th or 15th of the month. If you wait until the 15th of July to find out how you did in the month of June, it will be too late to make any of the needed corrections or changes.

Daily Sales

A study and comparison of daily sales will help to schedule employees efficiently, especially full-time employees. Daily sales are also a guide for purchasing and food preparation. Most places today do not carry any more inventory than needed, and watch food preparation closely to eliminate as much waste as possible. Daily sales records can also indicate which day will be best for closing, should you wish to shorten hours or days of operation to effect some needed payroll savings.

Meal Period Sales

Many operations keep records of total sales for each meal served: breakfast, lunch, dinner, late supper. Most of your sales are concentrated in these periods; it is important to know how much you are taking in during those specific times. It could be that it doesn't pay to open for breakfast—these records will show this. Comparison with past meal period sales may show that lunch or dinner sales are dropping, and something needs to be done to bring this back to normal. If you are only doing $500 for dinner and similar operations are taking in $1,000, it could be that you are not serving fast enough to realize your full potential—maybe you don't have enough seating to handle the crowd, or more than likely you don't have enough employees on duty at this rush period.

Hourly Sales

Most operations do not take hourly readings or keep a record of hourly sales because they think it is too much trouble. Hourly sales records can be very helpful in controlling wage costs and cutting down on wasted man hours. In fact, when places start keeping records of hourly sales, people are amazed to find out just how much or how little business they are actually doing at certain times of the day or night. Many places that are open 15 to 24 hours a day, seven days a week, will find after looking at this hourly sales record that during the slow or dead hours they are losing most of the money made in the few busy periods. Being open 24 hours a day may boost the total sales, but does not necessarily increase profits, especially if you have a lot of dead hours. With the shortage of skilled help and even unskilled employees it is difficult enough to staff a place for 12 hours a day, let alone 24. When you make out your weekly schedule of employees' hours, this hourly sales record can be a big help to actually tell you when man hours are or are not needed. Why bring in the dishwasher at 5 p.m. each night when the dinner business doesn't start until 6 p.m.?

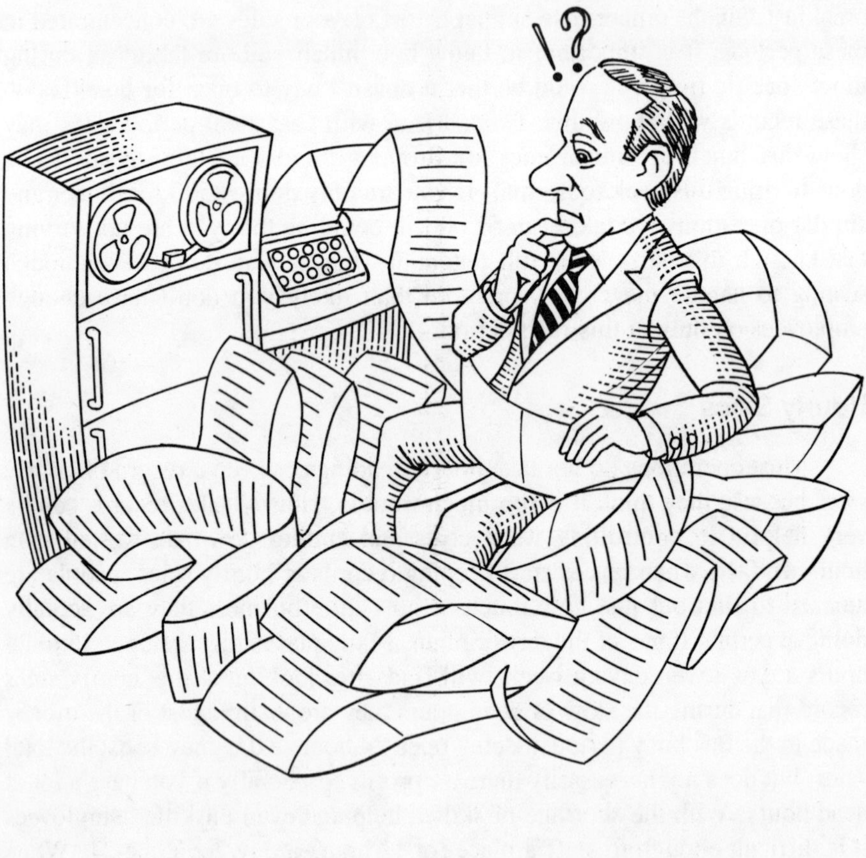

Departmental Sales

Some food service operations are expanding services to increase sales: they add bars, lounges, take-out, parties, banquets, and catering. This means more work, expense, and promotion to introduce all of these services. It would be wise to separate the sales of each of these functions so you can review them from time to time to determine their value in terms of the costs involved.

If you have a bar/lounge, and beverage sales are only 20 percent or more, it might pay to promote the sale of drinks to increase the profits—beverage sales can be very profitable. Perhaps some additional portable equipment could help you increase the potentially very profitable banquet and catering part of your total sales. Don't guess about the amount of sales you are making in the various activities; keep records so you will know!

Sales Per Employee Per Year

Most comparative figures on productivity in the retail field are expressed in dollar sales per employee per year. This can be a very useful figure for you to have to measure your performance against others in the food service industry, or even in other industries. This is not difficult to figure. Add all of your man hours for each week and divide by 40. This will give you the number of full-time employees you should have. For example, 420 man hours per week, divided by 40 hours, would mean 10½ full-time employees. Multiply by 52 weeks and you have the total man hours for the year. Divide this into the total yearly sales to arrive at sales per employee per year. If the national average is $20,000 per employee per year and you are only producing $15,000 per employee per year, then you are 25 percent below the average and need to take some action.

Sales Per Man Hour

Dollar sales, or meal sales if you are in certain kinds of institutional feeding, per man hour can be very valuable figures to show you how well you are really utilizing your help and facilities. If you are serving 360 school lunches per hour (6/minute) and another school is serving 600 lunches per hour (10/minute) then it would pay to study your operation and find out how service could be speeded up. If you have a chain, you can quickly compare the unit sales per man hour figures each day if you wish to determine the efficiency of different unit managers. If one unit is producing $14 per employee per hour, and another only $10 with the same facilities and prices, then you will know there is something wrong with the second unit. Looking back to the chart on page 11, "Sales Per Man Hour Needed to Produce Certain Wage Percent of Sales," you can quickly check your sales per man hour to know if you are going to get that percent of wage cost needed.

Sales Per Customer Per Check

The amount of sales per customer per check is a vital figure for a number of reasons. It is a good indication of where you stand in regard to the type of food service you have. It will also indicate the effects of price increases. If you start with an average check per person of $3.00, and raise menu prices but still get an average check per person of $3.00, it means that people are buying less expensive items on your menu and will still spend only $3.00 for what you are offering. This means that you really haven't gained anything from the price increases. A lower than average check per person means your menu, merchandising, or on-premise selling is not what it should be and you need more selling effort to increase check averages. If you are in the coffee shop class doing $3.00 average check per person, which is normal, but want to increase this figure to $4.00, you must change the format to that of a higher level operation that will justify the $4.00 average. The public is used to eating out now, knows prices, and has definite ideas on how much it will spend for certain items; people have limits and it is hard to exceed these in menu price increases.

Customer Counts

Though a customer count is not truly a sales figure, it does tell you how many people you are feeding. This figure will be valuable whether you are using meals or dollars as measurements. In prolonged inflationary periods, when there is one menu price change after another, sales will naturally increase. Often owners and managers will see these increased sales figures and be convinced that business is increasing, when actually the dollar sales increases are the result of the menu price increases only. In some cases you might actually have fewer customers because higher prices drive many away to other lower priced food service places (e.g. fast food operations) or force people to eat out less. Figures from the U.S. Department of Commerce reported in *Nation's Restaurant News* (August 8, 1979) demonstrate this point:

Commerce Dept. reports grocery sales outpace food service for first half of '79

WASHINGTON—Food service sales growth was outpaced by grocery store sales growth in the first half of 1979, according to U.S. Department of Commerce figures.

Grocery store sales were reported up a total 10.5% for the period, compared with the first half of 1978. But eating and drinking places' sales rose only 9.6%.

More significantly, by the height of the gas crisis in June, away-from-home eating sales showed only a 4.8% increase while grocery store sales jumped 11%.

It is important to realize that although some people are forced to eat out, there are those who can eat at home or carry their lunches when menu prices get too high. Add higher prices for gasoline to ever-increasing menu prices and you have two good reasons why more and more people will eat at home, causing those customer counts to drop even lower. Watch your customer counts closely; once you have lost customers it is very hard to get them back again, short of major changes in your place or extensive advertising and promotion programs.

Menu Tallies

Keeping menu tallies will help you in many ways. Briefly, this is a daily record of the number of the various items sold. More and more places are keeping and using menu tallies—the new electronic registers automatically tally items sold to give you not only total dollar sales, but also numbers of the various menu items. They even break them down into individual server's sales as well. Years ago, when we had to take handwritten checks and go through them one by one to make up the menu tallies, this job took hours of hard work and was not always accurate. If you have a huge menu, you do not need to total every item, but the tally should cover the main items, such as entrees and features. The new electronic registers have the capability of covering a great many items on your menu; you should be able to find a register to do your particular menu. You can use these figures in controlling purchasing, food preparation, pilferage, and cash receipts. For example, most cooks are not informed of the continuing sales of various menu items, and will prepare amounts of food based purely on what they think the sales are, or the size of the pot, kettle, or oven. The sales of an item can be dropping daily as a result of menu price increase, but the cook may go on making up the same amount for quite a while before the error is caught. Counts are also very useful in writing menus or making changes because they let you know which items are selling and exactly how many. This makes it possible to write a menu based not on your own personal likes or dislikes, but on actual sales and customer preference. Don't base your decisions on guesses by the cooks or servers, who will often answer "a lot" or "not many" when asked how many of a certain item customers are buying. Definitions of "a lot" or "not many" could vary by "quite a bit." Years ago I made a survey for a chain on the feasibility of putting in shake machines. Top management and even unit managers were convinced that they were selling "quite a few," but when we took some actual sales counts of the milk shakes sold, the average for all the units was about 15 shakes a day—hardly justifying the purchase of machines.

Menu Price Increases

As painful as price increases can be, it is wise to keep a record of all price increases and decreases and when they went into effect. This is not a difficult task. You should always have menus or signs reprinted instead of marking out the old prices and writing in the new—a practice that calls attention to the increase even with customers who did not know your old prices. In making a record of price changes you can either take a copy of an old menu, mark the date and indicate the price changes, or take the new menu, date it, and mark which items were raised. Keep this in your file; it is almost impossible to keep all of this information in your head or remember dates and amounts. When the time comes to put in some more price increases, you can pull out the record of the last increases, note the date and the items that were raised. Perhaps your menu tally counts will show that after you raised the price on the cheeseburger last May 15th, the sales fell sharply, so perhaps you had better not increase the price of this item again soon. By the same token, if you want to increase sales through price increases, it won't help much to increase some obscure item that has a daily tally of three or four.

Sales Per Server

Inasmuch as we consider productivity along with sales, it is a good idea to keep a record of sales produced by individual waiters/waitresses. As explained in the section on menu tallies, it is easier to get these individual sales from the computerized registers now being used. Because servers now receive wages and fringe benefits in addition to tips, we must consider their productivity along with that of other employees. They must be considered salespersons representing the owners and management directly to the customers. If they are not productive, making sales and rendering good service, then this is a matter of concern to management. A server whose sales (or checks written) are always below average needs more training or help from management or may not be suited to this type of work and should be replaced.

Comparative Increase/Decrease in Sales

In all of the various sales figures kept, the real value is in recording and keeping comparisons as you go (last week, same week last year, last month, same month last year, etc.) so you can tell where your business is headed. If you are having comparative decreases in all categories, then you could be in for some real trouble. Perhaps the decrease is only in one area, like breakfast, in which case you can check the breakfast business to see what has happened. Most chains and individual operations look for sales increases each year. In periods of price increases you should adjust your sales increases to the amount of the price increases to find out whether you are attracting more business or whether the increase was due solely to the menu increases. Decreasing sales are a sign of trouble ahead. You should try to increase sales either by adding to the operation, opening other units, or by greater productivity and attracting new business. Without some sort of effort to do better in sales, a business will gradually die. The natural attrition in your group of regular customers will catch up with you if nothing is done to bring in new ones.

SALES ANALYSIS

As can be seen by the 15 categories listed above, there is much more to sales than just a gross yearly figure. Not only must we follow all sales trends closely, but it is important to break them down so that they can be analyzed to shed light on what is really happening. When this variety of sales figures is available, not only are we warned in advance of what is happening to the business, but we can pinpoint areas of trouble and take corrective measures. These adjustments can be based on facts and figures, rather than on opinions or feelings which are not always accurate. It is easy to detect when a business is running into trouble; the problem is in locating the difficulty and applying the right remedy. Guessing at what the trouble may be can sometimes lead to more problems. Studying detailed sales figures can help you make the decisions you'll need to make in the following areas:

Prices

Records will show if your prices are below normal, and indicate which items to increase. If sales records indicate that you have already increased menu prices enough, then you should hold the line on prices while trying to find relief in other areas by increasing sales or cutting waste and costs.

Advertising/Promoting

Many companies carry on a continuous program of advertising and promotion to ensure keeping their sales high or adding to them. Others wait until the various sales figures indicate a drop-off, and then engage in some advertising and promotion to bring the figures up to normal. In either case, detailed sales figures will keep you posted and you will know when to act and why. It is better to step in fast to boost sagging sales and profits than to wait until they fall so low that you don't have enough money left for advertising and promotion.

Installing New Systems/Equipment

Those same detailed sales figures might also indicate that you have the customers needed but are not able to serve them fast enough at peak periods to generate the total sales needed. You can spot the trouble by the slow moving lines of people waiting to be seated. Perhaps the food is slow in coming from the kitchen; tables aren't being bused fast enough for new parties to be seated and served; waiters/waitresses are disorganized and are spending more time dashing around than actually serving; it takes too long to get the order and write the check; cooks can't process the checks in rotation, or guests can't get a check when ready to leave—in other words your system just isn't working smoothly to produce maximum sales during the peak periods. If you don't realize high sales at rush periods you certainly won't produce them at mid-morning and mid-afternoon when the place is empty. You can do some investigating on your own or call in professional people who can analyze and introduce new systems and equipment to speed your service and increase sales. Start in the dining room with that long waiting line and discover first hand what is holding up service by working your way back to the kitchen. Talk with your servers, cooks, and other employees. Many of them can tell you of specific problems so you can start some new and better systems. At least you'll be able to organize the confusion, if nothing else!

Menus

The successful menu fits the customers, the locations, and the employees. Careful analysis of the various sales figures (check averages and item tallies) allows you to tailor your menu specifically to your particular place. Perhaps you started off with the wrong items, at the wrong price levels, or had too many or too few items on the menu. You're not stuck with your mistakes. By studying the figures, you can reshape the menu gradually until it best suits you and your customers. In starting any new food service operation, it is necessary to more or less guess what items will be best on the menu, but after you have been in business for a while you'll have developed detailed sales records and can tell what items are not being accepted. Drop these and try others until the right menu is established.

Format

Many times new places are opened that just don't fit the location or surroundings. In other cases, a restaurant will do well at first and then business will start to taper off slowly, indicating that there will be real trouble in the future. Your sales figures may not tell you exactly what to do, but they *will* tell you that something is wrong and some action is needed. You may then try changing menu and price level, changing decor, or adding new features like a salad bar.

Expansion

Continued long waiting lines and high sales may indicate it is time to expand. If you don't do it, someone else will come by, see the full dining room and waiting lines, and open a place down the street. This is particularly true today. All someone has to do is open a place somewhere that looks as though it's busy, and before you know it, five or six more eating places are being built nearby.

INCREASING SALES

Most restaurant operators know their dollar sales, and whether they are going up or down. Most of the trade journal reports on the financial conditions of companies headline sales figures as a barometer of how the company is doing. If you assume the presidency of a company or become a manager, increasing sales will become one of your main concerns, whether it be total company sales or sales of one unit. Companies that have zero sales growth or have sales decreases are thought to be in trouble, or at least heading for financial problems. Companies need to expand and grow to meet rising costs and maintain a healthy financial posture. Costs and expenses can be cut, but they must be cut only so far, and then one must work to increase sales. Not only are high sales good for profits, but customers seem to like a busy place much better even though they must wait in line to be seated. Their theory seems to be, "Must be a good place with all of these people here." There are other advantages to operating a high-volume sales operation. It is easier to

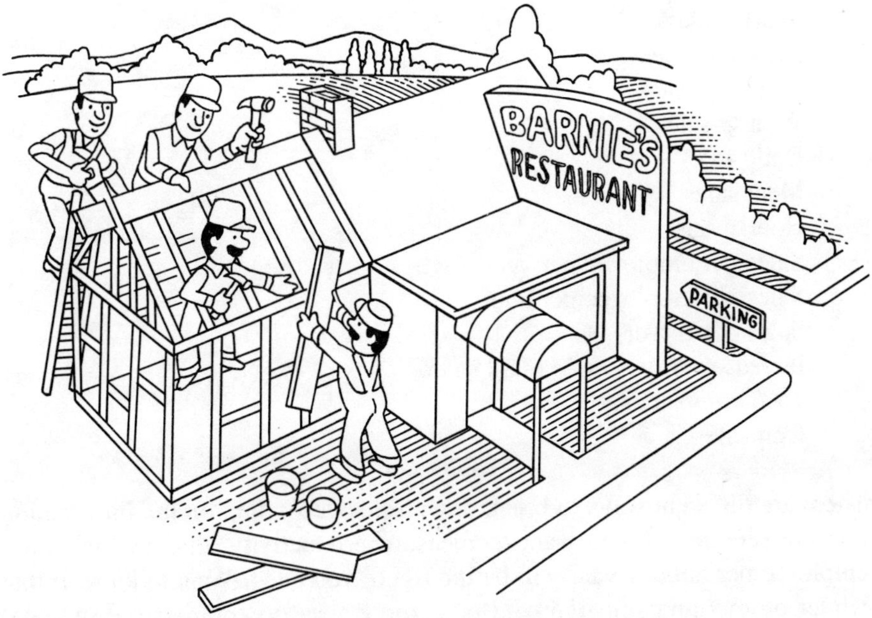
BARNIE'S
RESTAURANT
PARKING

manage because you can afford to hire the skilled key people needed to carry the load. The most difficult place to manage is one with little business, because the manager must wear many hats; busy places seem to run more smoothly. Strange to say, but you can get better service in a busy restaurant than in one that only has a few customers. Last but not least, since tips are the biggest part of servers' incomes, the busy place will attract the best servers.

If we want to come up with a thorough analysis of the business, we can break down the gross sales figure into several classifications:

    Yearly sales
    Seasonal sales
    Monthly sales
    Weekly sales
    Daily sales
    Meal sales
    Hourly sales
    Sales per employee per year
    Sales per employee per hour
    Sales per server
    Increases or decreases in all sales
    Total company sales
    Unit sales

There are different ways to break down sales depending on the information you are seeking. If you want to measure productivity, then the sales per employee per hour or year will be the figure you need. Want to know if that winter promotion campaign paid off? You'll need to compare the seasonal sales with last year's. A quick check of your peak dinner sales per hour will show if your service from the kitchen is really as fast as it should be, or whether it should be improved to increase sales and improve service. The sales figure quoted most often is the gross yearly sales, because this is the largest and will impress more people. In advertisements of restaurants for sale, the yearly sales figure is always quoted, even though a large yearly sales figure does not always mean a large net profit. This is why it is important to study all the sales figures to get the true picture. A study of the financial reports of some food service chains will show that some have declining profits despite increased sales. Other chains have declining sales yet show increased profits. Increased sales can be beneficial, as we all know, but if you don't have the proper control of the business, the increased profits that are supposed to result can be quickly eroded by waste and increasing costs. Many are overly enthusiastic when seeing increased sales. They go overboard on unneeded spending and expansion. The financially healthy business is well balanced in all parts of its operation, from continually increasing sales to higher profits and growth.

Let's look at some ideas and methods for increasing sales in the food service industry.

Increasing Menu Prices

Raising prices is still the easiest and most widely used way to increase sales in food service. Not only is this the easiest way to offset increasing costs by quickly passing them on to the customer, but increasing menu prices also results in the appearance of a temporary fast increase in sales. Many times menu price increases are instituted in response to a decrease in profits, but in other instances menu price increases are made in advance, on reports that costs will increase in the future. A bad frost in the orange groves on Friday can send the price of frozen concentrate up on the following Monday. Continuous menu price increase over a period of years can inflate sales and profits to the extent that what was once a rather low-profit industry can become one that is interesting to many investors and speculators. This is what is happening now, with the formation of many new chains and mergers and acquisitions by the large conglomerates.

On the other side of the coin, there are indications that the ever-increasing menu prices might run into difficulties despite the prevailing optimistic assumption that the boom is just getting started. An article in *Nation's Restaurant News* (August 20, 1979) has some interesting observations.

Decrease in real sales a signal to the industry
By Charles Bernstein

. . .[Statistics indicate] a sharp drop-off in food-service chain real sales for the second quarter. In addition, grocery store total sales growth is shown to be outpacing food-service total growth by an uncomfortable margin.

No doubt some in the industry will dispute these figures and claim they are "slanted" or "negative" or "damaging to the industry." It is possible to debate the figures endlessly. But the basic principles emerge clearly.

Food-service real sales did tail off sharply from April to June, and the gas shortages certainly had something to do with it. But so did average menu price rises listed industrywide at 11.2% between this June and last June. The customer simply is not standing for it—particularly when tough times hit, i.e., a gas shortage or a recession.

Why are grocery store sales not as badly affected? After all, their price increases in the past year have been in the range of food-service operators. It's apparent that the perception to the customer is quite different . . . that food-service operators have raised their prices more drastically and that the same price-value relationship isn't holding.

Hardest hit, according to the figures, are the basic fast-food burger chain and coffee shop chain segments. Price rises are more evident to the consumer in these categories. If a gourmet restaurant raises its price 10% so that a dinner becomes $22 instead of $20, that isn't likely to be noticed as much as a supposedly price-oriented $1.05 burger that jumps to $1.25, or any number of other items that are supposed to be "low-priced."

In short, the last thing anyone needs now is complacency or trying to blame Wall Street analysts for the legitimate problems facing the industry. They must be acknowledged and met head-on with an even stronger effort to control prices and keep a much closer eye on the entire value-price package.

The article points out that statistics indicate "a sharp drop-off in food service chain real sales for the second quarter. In addition, grocery store total sales growth is shown to be outpacing food service total growth by an uncomfortable margin." What this means is that the sharp menu price increases have convinced many that it is cheaper to eat at home. Many people are forced to eat out—they are the food service industry's captive audience—but most of the public who eat out do have other choices. If menu prices go too high, we will see a sharp decrease in customer counts. Most working Americans do not have automatic cost of living escalating wage contracts. They must absorb higher costs with a more or less stationary income. People cut out the frills first; eating out is a pleasant experience, but it is much more important to pay the rent or have money for gasoline.

The article also makes the point that the fast food chains and coffee shop segments are the hardest hit by the decreasing sales, because price increases in the lower categories are more noticeable. Years ago when coffee was selling for five cents it took a long time for the industry to get up the courage to raise it to ten cents (many went up only seven or eight cents), because this was immediately noticed by all, even though it was only a five cent increase.

Once you have raised prices, watch your customer counts and menu sales tallies closely to find out the public reaction. If the price increase is too high, you will quickly note a decrease in customer counts. This could of course translate into lower sales at a later date.

Quite a few years ago a certain chain was looking for higher sales and profits. One of the executives noted that they had sales in the millions on a certain item. His answer to more profit in a hurry was to raise the price of this item. Very simple: if 2,000,000 are sold in a year, raise the price ten cents and you will increase profit by $200,000. The problem was that after the price was raised, the sales of the item dropped to the point where the profit was the same or less. Sometimes raising the price of a profitable item on your menu will drive people to a lower priced item with a higher food cost, and you can end up losing money. When we raised the price of hamburgers one too many times many customers selected the lower priced hot dog instead. The hot dog not only had a lower price but a much higher food cost, so our net gain was zero.

No one can doubt that increasing selling prices has benefited many in food service. It is an easy way to increase sales and profits, but the safest course is to couple price increases with cost savings and higher productivity. The customer will pay for your waste and inefficiency only so long, and there will be resistance, which could result in lower sales and profits. It is tempting to raise prices when we read about restaurants getting $20 to $30 check averages and doing millions in sales each year, but it is important to remember that most customers still live on a budget and are looking for good value. The subject of price increases is also discussed in another article in *Nation's Restaurant News* (October 29, 1979), recommending that prices be hiked.

An expert's "shocker": hike prices

MIAMI BEACH—"The best thing the food-service industry can do is to increase prices."

That was the rather unconventional view expressed by marketing specialist Dan Nimer to food-service operators gathered for a pricing and positioning presentation at this year's Multi-Unit Food-Service Operators (MUFSO) conference sponsored by *Nation's Restaurant News*.

Nimer, president of a consulting firm specializing in planning, marketing and pricing strategy, cautioned operators about the current trend to roll back prices.

Price reductions, he said, could lead to a price war that would be devastating to the industry.

(After the presentation, Burger King executive vice president Chris Schoenleb said, "No price war is in the making. We're not that stupid.")

Nimer said the popular theory that decreasing prices will increase market share and compensate for the narrowed profit margin is "suicidal."

"This approach can only result in low-price, low-value suppliers," Nimer said, adding that prices should not be looked at as merely "a function of costs."

"Your costs are irrelevant to pricing strategy," Nimer said. "They are only important in making supply decisions and in telling you what your market is."

The customer, not costs, should be the price determinant under Nimer's alternative to conventional cost-oriented pricing strategy.

"You have to reverse your perspective and look at the marketplace first. Know your customer and let the price required to deliver the value expected by the customer lead to the prices instead of letting costs lead to price."

Quoting Peter Drucker's

thesis that the primary purpose of business is to create a customer, Nimer said that it is this customer that determines the price.

Once the customer's expectations of value and the relative price are determined, it is up to the operator to build his marketing plan around communication of value offered, he said.

"The only costs that can be regarded as relevant," Nimer said, "are those costs added to sustain or communicate the value."

Nimer concluded that his value-oriented strategy is the only way to increase bottom line in an industry whose profit margins are as sensitive to pricing as is food service.

"Boosting prices just 2% industrywide would effect a $2 billion increase in bottom line and a significantly improved return on investment," he said.

Food-service operators reacted strongly to Nimer's unconventional pricing strategy and his prediction of a price war.

"There will be no price war," Burger King's Schoenleb said. "We are not as stupid as Mr. Nimer thinks, particularly those of us in the hamburger segment."

Other operators expressed concern that implementing Nimer's theory would result in their pricing themselves out of the market.

This is yet another viewpoint on raising prices, in which an expert claims that prices should not be based on costs, but that it is the customer that determines the price. As with so many aspects of our industry, there is no hard and fast rule to apply to all places about price increasing. It should, however, be done very carefully; you must be sure to watch the customers' reactions.

Increasing Productivity

Increasing productivity is seldom thought of as a good way to increase sales, especially when a facility is already in operation. Because the food service industry ranks low among the major industries in productivity, we know that much can be done to improve in this area. The first part of this manual went into detail on ways to increase productivity:

Improving quality of employees
Reducing the amount of food preparation
Reducing hours and days of operation
Improving layout and equipment

In other words, many existing food service operations are not making the most of what they have, and as a result, their sales are not as high as they should be.

Just by going around and noting the long waiting lines at busy periods and knowing that customers' number one complaint is slow service, we can see that very few food service facilities are operating at top efficiency or maximum productivity. We also know the problem the food service industry has in getting and keeping good employees. Efforts to increase real productivity over the past years have been thwarted by the many menu price increases which gave the false impression that productivity had increased.

Once you start measuring your productivity on a regular basis, whether it be sales per employee per hour, day, or week, you can easily trace your actual performance to see if you are getting more efficient and productive. It won't take long to study the operation and make changes and improvements, once you know they are needed.

Many years ago, when car food service first started, we had a very complicated system. The carhop took the order, went into the service area and ordered and picked up each item, and next went to a cashier who checked each item and collected the money. The order was then delivered to the car. When the customer was finished, lights blinked and the same server had to return, collect the money, and pick up the tray. With such a system it was easy to see that a great number of carhops were needed, but since they worked for tips only, not much was done to improve the system.

There came a time when carhops were not as plentiful and had to be paid, so a system was needed to reduce the number needed and speed service. A new system was designed. The order was taken at the car, the carhop then pre-rang the check on a register that itemized and totaled the check. The pre-rung check was given to an assembly table where one person assembled the entire order. A pickup light was flashed and the carhop returned to pick up the complete order and pre-rung check. The order was delivered to the car and the money was collected in advance. This meant that when the customer was ready to leave anyone could remove the tray at once. At the end of the evening, each carhop paid the total of all his/her checks shown on the register instead of paying a cashier for each tray. The results of the new system were outstanding. Carhops went from writing and serving between $30 and $40 a night in checks to $200 or more. In some busy locations the number of carhops needed dropped from 60 to 75 to 12 to 15, while the customer enjoyed much faster service and the operation increased sales. This is an example of a change in the system that made a great difference. Later on the system was further refined so that the customers simply called in their orders to a central switchboard, which eliminated the necessity of carhops taking orders. Very often a series of small inexpensive improvements like these can make a substantial increase in productivity and sales.

Faster Service

Because there are so many complaints about slow service in the food service industry, it is important that we consider this in the search of ways to increase sales. If we can speed service in any way we will be accomplishing two things: making the customer happier, and increasing table turnover and sales. In either case we have nothing to lose and much to gain by putting forth effort in this direction. The key to understanding the importance of fast service to both customers and management is the realization that most want to eat at certain meal times. Most of your lunch business occurs in the 90-minute period between 12 noon and 1:30 p.m. If you have 200 seats properly balanced in deuces, fours, sixes, etc., then you will seat an average of 80-90 percent maximum, or 160 to 180 people. If you turn the dining room over one and one half times at lunch, you will feed 270 people, but if you turn the same dining room over two and one half times you will feed a maximum of 400 or more people. If your check average is $3.00, you will be realizing some $400 more for lunch each day, which could mean a lot in gross yearly sales and profits. We know the two-and-one-half-time turnover is possible because there are many places doing this much or even a little more each day.

What causes slow service? The same old basic reasons we have had for years and years—managers stick to the old concept of "cooking and preparation" as the most important part of the food service industry.

Service Orientation

First of all, to increase sales, management must become service oriented and realize the importance of good fast service. If management's prime concerns are purchasing, food preparation, and control, then being out in the dining area to supervise and speed service will be low on the list of priorities. It is evident that many in management do not regard service as important; we rarely see anyone from management out in the dining areas supervising or helping with the service. In fact, you very seldom see a chef supervising the service of his or her food. If management doesn't take a keen interest in service, then the employees are not going to put forth their best efforts. The first step then must be for management to be present, and direct at least the start of service at every serving period. This is the best way to make sure the customers are being served quickly and correctly. This applies equally to fast food, self-service, or table service. If the serving lines in cafeterias are not properly staffed and set up with food, then the number of people going through the line will be reduced, and sales will be lower. Fast food operations must be thoroughly set up to take care of those rush periods, otherwise they lose a lot of important sales. It is vital that owners and management realize the importance of fast service right from the start, otherwise the operation will always have problems in reaching its sales potential. Many busy operations could increase sales by ten percent or more if someone would acknowledge the importance of fast service and do something about it.

Equipped for Fast Service

Very few food service operations are really equipped or designed for fast service and high seat turnovers during the rush periods. So much emphasis has been and still is being placed on cooking and preparation, that little attention is paid to the service equipment and facilities. In many cases, the decorator will not permit service stands in or near the dining areas because they detract from the decor, so the servers must take quite a trip each time a piece of flatware, coffee, or a glass of water is needed.

The typical planning for an operation might end up something like this, for a 200-plus seat restaurant with bar and lounge. First the kitchen, storage areas, and dining areas are planned, squeezing in as many seats as possible. The same goes for the bar/lounge, with as many stools at the bar as possible,

Increasing Productivity and Sales 71

and very crowded lounge seating. Assuming that there will be two to three service cooks and one or two bartenders, the amount of equipment and space they receive will often be disproportionately large. The dishroom will be shoved back into a remote corner to hide it from view, despite the fact that this will make it very hard to get soiled ware to it and clean ware back to the points of use. Now that all this has been planned, we come to the service facilities for the waiters, waitresses, and bar servers. Two hundred seats in the dining areas could mean as many as ten servers plus bus help for the rush period. Fifty to 60 seats in the lounge and bar could mean two or three servers there in addition. If we are lucky we can squeeze in one or two service stands measuring four by six feet for the food servers, while the people serving drinks (both the dining room and lounge servers) will have to work in a space two by four feet at the bar, created by removing one or two bar stools. In short, the servers, who outnumber the cooks and bartenders by three or four to one, must work in and get everything they need from service areas that are far too small.

Very few in our business have ever carefully studied the problems and logistics of service in detail, or they would know that there are at least 50 or more items needed in the service of food. This number can become much larger as the service becomes more elaborate. Napkins, ice, water, coffee, cream, sugar, iced tea, milk, Sanka, four to ten kinds of glasses, plates, saucers, butter condiments, doilies—the list of items that the servers must have on hand to give good service goes on and on. Actually the servers need many more items on hand than the cooks, and should have more space allocated. If you think you can get all of these items in the quantities needed to serve a 200-seat dining area on a six-foot service stand, you are really dreaming. This explains why five minutes after the meal period starts there is a mad rush to find a spoon, cup, glass, or some other item needed for service. The same applies to the service kitchen. If space hasn't been provided for the plates, platters, underliners, casseroles, and food, the cook will look silly standing with a cooked steak and no plate or platter to put it on. That special apple pie you feature and spend hours making will never get to the customer if the server can't find a clean plate and a fork, or if the warewashing system is so bad that it takes forever to get the tables cleared so you can serve the dessert. If you had the proper service bar setup, with enough space so that the servers could get their own glasses, ice, and mixers, and also wash their own glasses with an automatic glass washer, perhaps you would need only one bartender instead of two. This means the bar itself could be much smaller and more efficient, and you could speed the service of drinks by ten percent or more. It is hard to get the attention of servers in crowded bars and lounges and it takes time to get the drinks when the bartenders are stuck. Many orders for that second drink are missed because the guests don't have the time to wait or the servers just can't handle the business.

Consider the problem of warehandling for a moment. Here is a part of our business that is really ignored. Most think of it as a minor function, and place it on the bottom of the list in planning. "Stick it anywhere, just so you get it out of the way." "Make it fit in that corner we have left because it is such a mess," is the attitude management often takes. In terms of work and efforts, warehandling is one of the single biggest jobs you have. Think of the work of getting all those items to points of use, then to the tables, then returned to the sorting/washing area, and finally back to point of use again. If you don't have a good warehandling system, with the sort and wash area conveniently located, you are in for a lot of extra work, breakage, and what is most important, some hectic but slow service. If there isn't something clean to serve the food or drinks in or on, then you can't get them to the customer. It's like taking a large army to the front lines to meet the enemy and forgetting the guns and ammunition. If you can't remove the soiled ware quickly from the tables for the next course or party and get it back to the wash area, then you are at another standstill. If servers can't get food from the kitchen and drinks from the bar, then you will have a lot of occupied seats and tables producing little or no revenue. Not only do poor service facilities and equipment slow service, cut turnover, and reduce potential sales, but they seriously affect the quality of your service. Frustrated servers dashing madly about trying to get food and drinks are in no position to give fast and efficient service. Perhaps management is unable to notice these problems, but you can rest assured that the paying customers are well aware of the situation when they don't get friendly service from harried servers. Waiting in line for what seems like hours; waiting at the tables for long periods; getting poor service, like coffee with no cream or spoon; being unable to get the check when ready to leave, will not leave customers enthusiastic about your restaurant. It will do little toward building business and increasing sales. Don't assume, as many do, that your service is tops, but actually check your dining areas and see how fast and well your customers are being served. You don't need to be an expert to note long waiting lines that do not move or nervous guests sitting at tables waiting for some kind of service. Fifteen or twenty minutes spent in the serving kitchen can tell anyone whether the food and other items are coming out smoothly or if there is bedlam and confusion.

One of the best ways to find out what could be slowing your service is to sit down and talk with your employees. If yours is a table service operation, the servers must depend on tips for most of their income; they will be keenly aware of problems that reduce the number of customers they can handle at a given time. Many places today make use of an expediter during busy periods to speed service and personally direct the operation. An expediter can be the manager or some other designated person who is out front at the start of the busy periods and takes direct charge of the entire operation. He or she directly supervises the servers, cooks, and all other personnel until the crush has subsided. Often the expediter takes checks from the servers and calls in the orders to the kitchen. Then he/she makes sure the servers pick up the orders and serve them quickly. The job is much like being a quarterback on a football team, who not only calls the plays but sees that they are properly executed.

The expediter begins working before the rush by checking all departments and personnel to make sure everything is set up and ready. Watch a manager in a McDonald's during a busy period and see how he/she controls the entire operation from behind the counter in the front of the store. He/she is the one who notes which foods are ready and what is needed, and gives the verbal orders to the kitchen. This eliminates all the confusion and shouting that occur when no one in authority is present. If you want to speed up your service, try this system. You'll get the most cooperation from the whole crew with a minimum of noise and confusion.

Another way to speed service and get the maximum number of customers served during those few rush hours is to follow the Boy Scout motto: *"Be Prepared."* In many operations, whether it be fast food, self-service, or table service, not being set up and ready to do business is one of the biggest weaknesses; it causes untold lost sales and customers. If you are open all day and night, there will be three busy periods to prepare for: breakfast, lunch, and dinner. This is the most difficult type of place to run, because just as soon as one rush is over, you must get ready for the next. Employees would rather rest in between rushes than think about getting ready for the next group of customers. Operations that serve only lunch and dinner have less of a problem, while places that serve only dinner have just one rush period to prepare for.

If you do not prepare adequately for a rush period you may find yourself "stuck." Very simply this means that the whole system has almost come to a halt; little or nothing is coming from the kitchen and very few customers are being served. In my own experience, although meal periods with customers lined up and cooks and servers running madly about appear to indicate large sales, at the end of the so-called rush under such circumstances the sales were low, because very few people were getting served. On other days when we were well prepared, and everything went quietly and smoothly, surprisingly the sales were much higher!

Take the time to study your service system. Observe systems used by others to speed service and increase customer counts and sales.

Menu Adjustment

In addition to raising or lowering prices to increase sales and profits, it is also possible to change the menus or format to attract new business. Part of an article that appeared in *Nation's Restaurant News* (August 20, 1979) is reprinted to show how one chain did counteract decreasing sales.

As sales plummet, Wendy's expands its menu
By Ron Fink

DUBLIN, Ohio—Trying to stem a severe decline in store traffic, Wendy's is stepping up local marketing efforts, experimenting with salad bars and planning to expand its breakfast test.

The 1,620-unit chain is also slowing expansion slightly and aggressively seeking to reacquire franchised stores.

The moves follow a 23% decline in real sales for company stores for the second quarter, compared to the same period the previous year. For the quarter ended June 30, Wendy's average store sales fell 11.7% on a systemwide basis without making allowances for price increases, according to William Leiter, vice president of finance.

In company stores alone, average volume declined 7.9% from the same period last year, Leiter said. Taking into account the chain's 15% year-to-year price hike, company store real sales for the quarter were down 22.9%.

In response, the chain

based here has reassessed its marketing strategy and decided to place increased emphasis on local store promotion and less on national advertising during the second half of the year, according to Wendy's vice president of marketing, Jay Schloemer.

At the same time, Wendy's has unveiled its first salad bar in Delaware, Ohio, and plans to roll out its experimental breakfast menu, now in one unit in Lancaster, Ohio, to 11 units in the Toledo market by Sept. 1.

Wendy's decided that such things as breakfast menus and salad bars were indicated to boost sagging sales. The article goes on to say that they were not doing enough dinner business; naturally it is difficult to operate with only a busy luncheon period. Other chains have gone to 24-hour-a-day operation, seven days a week, adding late night menus to attract more business. Many watch the various national menu surveys and then add the items ranked as most popular to their own menus. Others in the industry adjust menus to achieve higher check averages. For years McDonald's served the regular sized hamburger. The quarter pounder which they later came out with gave them a higher check average. Now they and others are coming out with larger and more expensive sandwiches in an effort to take the check average up a little higher. Adding salad bars in many chains has been another attempt to add to the check average and increase the take. Many add desserts to get the customer to spend more money.

Some, of course, have added too many items to their menus in an effort to get more customers and increase sales. In fact, some chains added new items so fast that they soon went out of business because the menu became too varied and the employees couldn't handle it. It is fine to add pizza, Mexican foods, fried chicken, submarines, thin-sliced roast beef sandwiches, salad bars, breakfasts, or any other sales leader on the most recent menu polls, but make sure you can handle the item with your present layout, equipment, and employees. When Arby's first came out with the thin-sliced roast beef sandwich, it wasn't long before many in the industry were also serving thin-sliced roast beef sandwiches, but most had little success. Remember, specialty places are designed and equipped to handle the item featured. They not only can prepare and serve the item correctly, but quickly as well. It takes more than a small fryer shoved into an already overcrowded kitchen to serve fried chicken right, as many have learned to their sorrow.

Every operation should run a continuous menu tally on items sold to determine which items are and are not selling. Menu changes will be needed from time to time, because customer tastes change and it is necessary to add new items. These same tallies will show which items are not selling; it would be advisable to drop these items to avoid waste and needless preparation. No one can write the perfect menu for you, but over a period of time it is possible to come up with the selection of items best suited to your customers and facility. It is not always the huge menu with countless selections that is the winner. It can be much better to serve fewer items if you can serve them well and fast. Many of the busiest restaurants have small, one-sheet menus, and find that three- or four-page menus do not seem to be as effective.

Realize Existing Potential

The real challenge in food service is to make the most of a given place and location. It is very interesting to watch the growth of restaurants and other food service operations that start with little or nothing, but with imagination and a little creativity do millions in sales after relatively few years in business. Naturally not all have the same measure of success, but it proves beyond a doubt that it is possible.

When we go to restaurants in obscure locations that are doing big business, we often wonder why people would travel from far away to go there. An article in *Nation's Restaurant News* (October 29, 1979), reprinted here, provides one explanation of the success and ability to attract business year after year that some restaurants have.

Restaurants' role defined: Quality foods count the most
By Cecilia Brancato

MIAMI BEACH—Stimulate the customer with new foods and exciting presentations of those foods and the restaurant becomes a vibrant, living gathering place.

That's what a panel of industry experts gathered for the Multi-Unit Food Service Operators (MUFSO) conference on food and beverage want their restaurants to be like and that's what they see as the trend for restaurants in the 1980's.

There will be more emphasis on the customers—making them want to come back. Price and design will be secondary to food and the presentation of meals, the panelists said.

"People forget what a place of hospitality is supposed to be," said Michael Hurst, vice president of Marina Bay in Fort Lauderdale and co-moderator of the panel.

"It's a vibrant, living thing—a gathering place. How do you give a place life? Through the food or the product and through promotion. We must give more than just a dining experience. We must give away fun and excitement," Hurst said.

Fun and excitement is delivered in a variety of packages.

Joseph F. W. Gardiner, senior vice president of food and beverage for Hilton Hotels, created "a food fantasy"—a self-service, multiple choice, elaborate display of food in Hilton Hotel restaurants that turn a meal into a "happening, an event."

Hilton creates different countries and cities at its banquets through theatrics. "It all adds up to show biz," Gardiner said.

Jorgen Moller, owner of Prince Hamlet Danish Restaurants in Miami, turned Sundays and Thursdays into complimentary crepe nights at which customers make their own desserts with a variety of fillings.

"What am I doing? Spending $30 to $40 for the crepes but making people happy. I might kill my dessert sales, but I'm bringing in a lot of business," Moller said.

"The most important thing to me is bodies in chairs—to get them there and to keep them there," Moller said. He came to Miami in 1969 and now operates a $3 million business.

Color coordination and arrangement of food is one way of exciting customers, said Raymond Marshall, board chairman of Acapulco y Los Arcos Restaurants in California. Complement the green hue of avocado with red tomatoes and black pitted olives, he said.

Give the consumer an unusual item even if it doesn't sell too well, Hurst said. "You'll get a ton of conversation."

It's the reason Hurst has begun to offer french-fried alligator strips.

"Your own customer will become your salesman if you give him something to talk about," Hurst said.

And when you give the customer something to talk about, don't tell him about it on a napkin or a piece of paper, he said. Teach your staff to sell it, to verbalize, to talk about why it's different and then inspect to ensure it's being done.

"You must give them something exciting and new and they will talk," he said.

Hurst opened his Marina Bay restaurant and club six years ago and designed it to capture the tropical experience of south Florida. It consists of a floating club, restaurant and hotel.

His attention to creating and stimulating fun in his operations is depicted in his presentation of foods—an "extremely important" factor in terms of product.

When his restaurants serve fish stew the pot is brought out smoking and steaming and an aroma of herbs and spices tantalized the customers.

"The smoking Florida stew is part of the pizzazz," Hurst said. And it entices others to order the stew. "Give the customers something for nothing. Give them fun and excitement."

There is no single formula that you can apply for instant success in food service, but the popular places do have something in common—attention to the likes and dislikes of the customers. Again, we are engaged in food service and that means giving the customer what he or she wants. This is what brings people back to spend money and produce those huge sales figures.

Next in importance to service is *selling*. Whether it be a fast food operation on campus, a cafeteria, or a gourmet restaurant, all must attract customers and sell once the customer is aboard. Every possible avenue must be explored to realize the maximum potential of a particular location. One operator quoted in the article printed above sums it all up in a very few words: "The most important thing for me is bodies in chairs—to get them there and keep them there." If you don't get the customers in the first place, it will be hard to sell. Once you do get them, you'd better have something good to offer to keep them coming. Unfortunately we are seeing a period of rapid chain expansion in which new eating places are being turned out like cars on an assembly line. Then standard features lack personality and offer the diner little or no excitement. Along with emphasizing personal selling and creativity, operators can develop additional features to attract more customers and build sales.

Bar/Lounge

If your operation has neither a bar nor a lounge, you could find one or both of these a profitable addition. Considering that liquor costs can run as low or lower than 25 percent and bar payrolls as low as seven to ten percent, it is easy to see how this could be the most profitable part of any food service operation. The ratio of bar sales to food sales or to total sales will run from ten to 30 percent or more for places that really push drink sales. Many years ago there was a standing joke about restaurants that had 50 seats in the dining areas and 100 seats in the cocktail lounge, with at least an hour's wait for a table. Of course the customer spent that hour in the cocktail lounge having a drink or two. Many places that have bars and lounges fail to promote these features along with the service of food. In fact, I have been in places where the customer must ask if drinks are served. The sale of liquor and wine can be promoted on the menu and by wine lists, but the best results can be obtained by personal selling. Nothing beats: "May I serve you one of our famous martinis before dinner?" or "What wine would you prefer with your dinner?"

Party and Banquet

Setting up facilities for parties and banquets is another way to increase sales, make full use of space, and fill in some of those dead times. Many operations, particularly hotels and motels, are designed to take care of parties and banquets. They have special rooms and equipment to handle this type of business. It can be very profitable because the operator knows in advance how many guests there will be and what will be served. Many food service operations are designing layouts that can be adapted to parties and banquets. Dining areas are divided into two or more rooms that can be closed off to accommodate parties during the slower periods, but can still be operated at full capacity during normal busy times. For most places the promotion of parties and banquets can lead to profitable additions to sales that will not interfere with the regular business. The extra help needed over and above the regular crew can be part-time help on call when needed. Much of the promotion for parties and banquets can be "on premise," using table tents, special menu inserts, or attractive signs placed in the lobby and entrance. This additional service can also be mentioned in the classified telephone directory. Serving a banquet for 100 on a normally slow Monday or Tuesday night can do wonders toward boosting the sales for the week.

Catering/Take-out

If the customers don't have time to eat in your dining areas, or would rather eat at home, then set up a service so that they can take your food home or have it delivered to them. This is another way to make full use of a food service facility and realize maximum sales. Here again you are enjoying "found" business; if it is handled right, it will not interfere with your regular business. A large percentage of the fast food business is take-out. Now many are putting in "drive-through service" where the customer drives up, gives the order and picks it up without leaving the car. By studying your regular menu you can select the best items for take-out and make up a special menu. If you want to build this business there are several bits of advice:

Designate an area where customers can come in and place their take-out orders quickly. This can be the cashier station or somewhere near the kitchen.

Provide the necessary paper or styrofoam containers, bags, lids, and condiments where they will be needed. Have all these items readily available so the orders can be filled quickly. People who want take-out service are usually in a hurry, so the faster they can be served the better.

Don't make the mistake of charging extra for take-out. Many feel that they should charge for the paper goods and containers, but actually you will make just as much money as if the customer sat in the dining area, took up space for 20 or 30 minutes, and required service.

Take-out business can also be promoted on premise with special notices on your menu, signs drawing attention to the take-out area, and just the sight of people taking out bags and boxes of food. Many places print special small take-out menus that can be included with each order taken out, giving location and phone number. This allows customers to call in and place orders in advance and avoid long waits. People are well accustomed now to taking food home or to the office or car when they do not have the time to eat in a restaurant and do not want to prepare the food themselves. This has developed into a very large market. Most food service operators can get a piece of this business with very little effort and investment. If they can't come to your place of business to eat, feed them where they are!

Early Bird Promotion

Many places are promoting early dinner business by giving discounts or special prices from 4:30 p.m. to 6:00. (The exact time could be varied to suit your operation.) Some have printed special lower priced menus for this specified time. As was mentioned before, it is good business to fill those seats and keep them filled. For most places dinner business doesn't really start until 6:30 p.m. or later. Those several dead hours preceding could be turned into profitable business. Think of the millions of senior citizens who would like to eat out if the prices were a little lower. These people are glad to come early and enjoy a discount. This promotional idea started with the "happy hours" for bars that give special low prices on drinks from 4:30 p.m. to 6:00 p.m. to add some extra business during those slow times. Some other places just have one special food item each night for the early bird special, but even this limited choice seems to bring in business. If you have a bar there is always the chance that these customers will buy a drink, which will help your profits even more. It's hard to lose on this kind of promotion. Most who have tried it are very pleased with the increased sales and profits. It's much like special discounts that airlines give on certain flights that might otherwise have been only half filled. Since the planes must be flown with a full crew and would have the same costs, airlines choose to fill the seats and make some extra profits.

Special Nights

Special feature nights can be very helpful in building sales and profits. Again, this is a way to build business in the slow periods. Every operation knows from its sales records when the business is slow and needs promotion. Years ago a large chain did an excellent job with a one dollar all-you-can-eat fish fry every Wednesday night. All you could eat for one dollar would seem like a sure loser, but statistics showed that this promotion brought in hundreds of extra people per unit, making Wednesday night the biggest and most profitable night of the week. In addition, all of these people bought other things as well as the special. One thing that helps the volume and profits when you serve one item like this is that everyone can concentrate on just one entree. The service is very fast and a lot of people can be served in a very short time. Large volume business with no waste and high turnover can be profitable even though you are serving for a lower price.

On-Premise Promotion

Every time we think of promotion and advertising our minds turn to television, radio, or newspapers. However many fail to sell to the customers who are already in the place or "on premise." The first step to increasing sales in this way is to make the customer who is there want to come back. After this has been accomplished, then you can start on the off-premise promoting. The first job is to sell your place to the customer. If you have an attractive sign, well-maintained building with landscaped grounds, and an attractive entrance with a waiting area, you have come a long way toward making the guest feel he/she has come to the right place. The first impression is very important to customers, especially if they have never been to your place before. A broken sign, dirty windows, trash on the sidewalk, or dirty vestibules and rest rooms can put someone off long before they get to the table. Perhaps your regular guests may know that despite your poor housekeeping you *do* serve fairly good food, but that person about to enter for the first time doesn't know this, and a bad first impression can send him/her somewhere else in a hurry. Many times when people travel and stop at a strange restaurant, one member of the group or family will get out and take a quick look before the others come in to eat. If your place is attractive and inviting, the report on the quick look will be favorable, and can mean more sales for you.

Once the customer has entered it is up to you to sell food, beverages, or whatever else you have to offer. In some restaurants so much attention is paid to the decor it is hard to tell if you are in a restaurant, furniture store, or art gallery. Food can be sold by menu alone, but most people find it an attractive commodity; it lends itself to display and suggestive selling. Time after time people will see an exotic drink, delicious appetizer, or elegant dessert and order the same thing. "Bring me one of those" is heard very often where the product is shown. Sometimes our eyes are bigger than our stomachs; this is certainly true when we see food attractively displayed. It pays to advertise. It is much easier to sell anything if you show it well to the prospective buyer.

Buffets

Self-service buffets are becoming more popular even in the high-priced resort hotels. People like seeing these attractive displays of food and selecting exactly what they want. In many places you can return for more and this appeals to people as a chance to get something for nothing. With buffets you can combine table- and self-service to a degree that is pleasing to the guest while really speeding up service and increasing turnover and sales. I once did some remodeling designing for a very popular resort where thousands were being fed each day from a kitchen and dining room that had been designed to feed hundreds, using table service only. They had found a solution in the use of a very attractive buffet service for breakfast, lunch, and dinner. Guests could get table service if desired, but over 75 percent of them chose the buffet. There was table service for drinks and desserts, but it was amazing to see how quickly people were served with a minimum of help. If you are looking for a way to increase sales and handle a huge number of customers, think "buffet" as many are doing today.

Salad Bars

More and more places are turning to salad bars to draw more customers and increase sales and check averages. Several fast food chains have added salad bars at night to help bring in dinner business. Guests find it an attractive feature, because once again it incorporates the idea of going back to get "something for nothing." Then too people seem to enjoy putting together their own salads with dressings, especially if there is a large selection of items. This also gives the customer something to do while waiting for the entree to be prepared and served, making it easier on the server. This display can be most attractive and pleasing. The Prince Hamlet Restaurant in Miami, Florida, has built a multi-million dollar business by setting up elaborate appetizer and salad bars serving everything possible to guests, who can come back as often as they please. When you walk into the Prince Hamlet you see the food displayed very attractively. You *know* you are in a restaurant. Nothing sells food like displaying it; *that* is our business, not selling furniture and pictures.

Dessert Carts

The usual approach to selling desserts is to have the harried server ask, "You folks want some dessert?" or "If you want dessert, I'll bring you the dessert menu." In most cases the server is not too interested in serving dessert because it means additional time taking the order, clearing the table, and

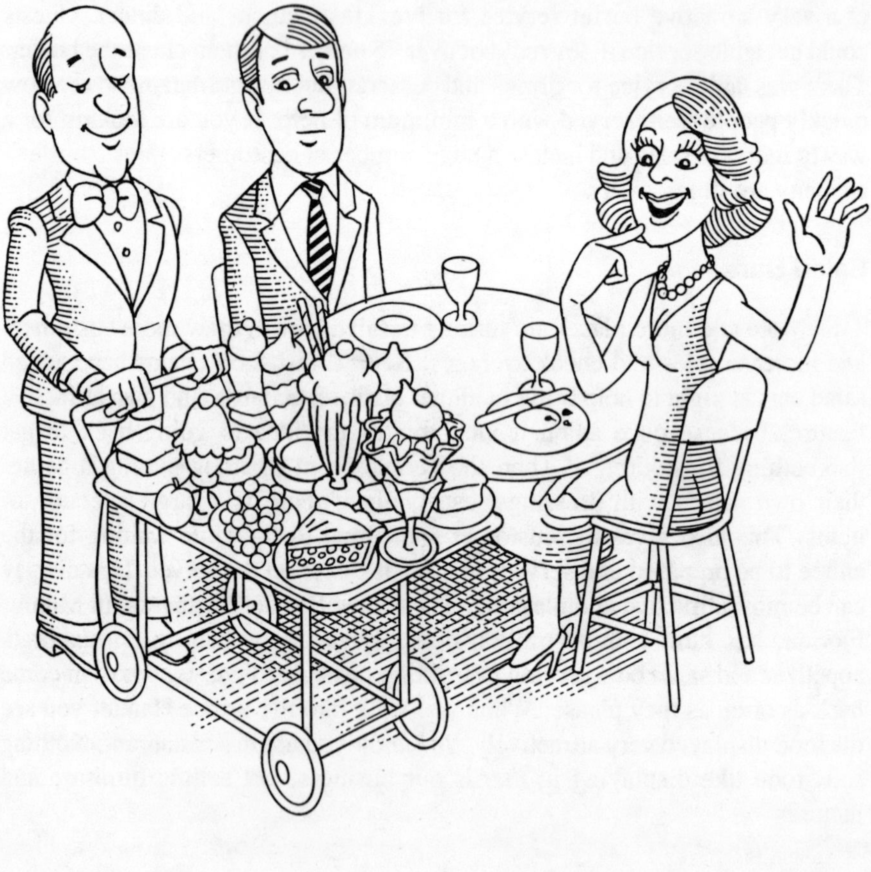

bringing more coffee, while it delays the seating of a new party. Then too, it is doubtful whether the sale of dessert will increase the tip, although it will increase the check average for management. Many places now do not push desserts because they would rather sell drinks before the meal, serve the entree, and move the people out quickly so the next party can be seated. This can promote high turnover and more sales, especially if you have a large business and waiting lines. However, if you want to sell desserts and increase check averages and sales that way, then dessert carts or attractive displays are the best ways to promote this business. No amount of description can do justice to a luscious chocolate cake or colorful ice cream parfait. Some time ago I visited a busy restaurant out West. As you walked in the door, you saw the beautiful display of their featured dessert, which was strawberry shortcake. Platters of hot biscuits, bowls of fresh strawberries and thick whipped cream were temptingly laid out. Before you were even seated you knew that you were going to have strawberry shortcake for dessert. Do I want a dessert after eating a filling entree? I may not be too keen on the idea, but if I see something that really looks good, my eyes will overrule my stomach every time!

Personal Selling

Perhaps the biggest weakness in American retail business as a whole is the lack of personal selling. After years and years of boom times we find ourselves in the position where people buy and there is little need to "sell" to stay in business and make huge profits. Walk into most car dealerships and you will be lucky if someone from the sales department approaches you, let alone asks you if you are interested in a new car. Today we are just supposed to buy without any questions or selling technique, explanation, or demonstration. So many of our retail outlets now are self-service; the customer walks around to find what he/she wants (or reasonable facsimile) and then has a problem finding someone to take the money or credit card. I am afraid this attitude has invaded the food service business to a considerable extent.

The possibilities of personal selling and good direct handling of customers are very important to increasing sales and check averages. Think of the times you have visited places where your only thought was to leave as soon as possible because of the treatment received. Getting the first drink was difficult and the second impossible; the server was definitely in a hurry so you skipped the appetizer and dessert and hoped that you would be fortunate enough to get the check and find someone to take payment. In many places not only do you order the minimum to avoid all the difficulties in service but you get the feeling that your business is not really appreciated. Greeting and personal selling in most food service operations is about as minimal as you can get. In most cases the sales and personal contact can be recapitulated in a few terse comments:

"How many in your party?"
"This way please."
"Your waiter/waitress will take your order."
"Are you ready to order?"
"Do you want dessert?"
"Sorry, this isn't my table!"

Most of this comes from years of "boom" business and customers gradually learning to just "buy" hoping someone will just furnish the product or the service.

What about tipping? Surely we have tipping to reward people for service over and above the average. This practice certainly ought to ensure good service since servers must get good tips to make a high income. Wrong again. Today you are expected to tip regardless of the service received. That 10-20 percent tip is as standard as the sales tax. Are servers the sales people they are supposed to be? It is important to realize at this point that your servers are about your only direct contact with your customer! If they fail to sell, who *will* do the selling to raise check averages and total sales? The attitude of many servers is, the less selling the better. They figure tips on the number of parties served. Selling that second drink or a dessert will mean the party will stay longer and reduce the number served during a particular time. After all, a certain number of customers will tip very little; servers feel they must rely on quantity to provide good average tip income.

As long as the boom continues and the public is satisfied with poor treatment, there is no real reason to extend yourself to make a living, but if you are interested in increasing sales and stealing a march on your competitors, then give personal selling a try.

Keep track of how much in sales each of your servers produces day to day. Who is the best sales person among all of your servers? Who is the worst, and needs help from management or replacement? If you are looking for a way to increase your sales, don't overlook the fact that your servers are supposed to be *sales persons*, not just people who deliver food to the tables and remove the soiled dishes. Your customers are human beings who enjoy recognition and good treatment. Who knows, with a little effort on the part of the sellers, some of these customers might spend more and come back more often. As for the servers, maybe some of those people who just never tip might consider giving a gratuity if the service were a little better. Taking customers and tips for granted is a way to lose both.

Off-Premise Promotion

The food service industry has greatly stepped up off-premise promotion and advertising in recent years. Much of this is being spent on television advertising by the chains, particularly the fast food chains. McDonald's now ranks third in spending on advertising of all the companies in the United States. The chains also use other media for this advertising such as radio, newspapers, and billboards, but television seems to be getting the biggest share of attention. When you realize that McDonald's is spending over 100 million dollars a year on advertising, there can be little doubt that they must find that the results are worth it. There are several factors to consider in launching a successful off-premise promotion program regardless of the medium selected:

Affording the Expense

Advertising is expensive. In considering it, the first requirement is that you can afford to lay out the kind of money necessary to build sales and profits. Many think of advertising as a means of pulling a weak, rundown business out of the red and into the profit column. This has been done in some cases, but the bulk of advertising and promotion is done by successful companies who want to further increase their sales and get ahead of competition. In other words, it may make most sense to engage in large-scale advertising if your operation is a success to start with. A company that is losing money will find it hard to find enough money to launch a big advertising program. Many will ask, "Why advertise if you are already successful?" The answer is: "To stay successful!" The public has a short memory. If you don't keep in touch with it you could lose a lot of business.

Doing a Good Job

In addition to being financially fit, it is also important to be sure that you are doing a good job of serving the public before starting an advertising campaign. Is your place (or places) in the kind of physical condition that will make it attractive to new customers? Are you serving good food? Is your service good enough to advertise? Unless you want to take part in false advertising, it would pay to step back and take a good look at your establishment and the kind of job you are doing. Good advertising programs will bring in more business, but if you are not offering good food and good service now, the customer will soon find this out. In a short time all the money spent for promotion will amount to nothing. You may get a short-lived burst of new business from a big campaign, but sooner or later the public will turn to other places that are offering more.

Something to Sell

Many advertising programs are successful, while others do not accomplish much. One of the main requirements for successful advertising is to have something definite to sell. Ads proclaiming "Good Food," "Good Service," "Open 24 Hours," or "Steaks and Seafood" are very general in nature and could apply to any food service operator's claims. If restaurant XYZ is advertising, "XYZ is the place to eat—our service is the best," this would not induce me to eat at XYZ rather than ABC. The successful advertisers offer something special to attract the public. Large grocery chains each week offer specific price reductions on certain items to attract the shoppers. McDonald's zeros in on one food item or a specific feature in each promotion to give the customer a definite reason for going there.

Handle the Business

One of the biggest mistakes in advertising and promotion is not being able to handle the business once it does come. Many mount a very fine advertising campaign and forget to beef up the work force, inventories, and all the other things needed to take care of the added business. There are others who want to play the "wait and see" game. They start the campaign and see if it does bring in more customers. If more business comes, then they start to worry about adding more employees, supplies, etc. Granted, this seems like the safe way to handle the situation. However, if you don't prepare in advance for the increased business, it will be difficult to handle it when it does come. The outcome of this delay strategy is that your inability to deliver the product or service will cause you to not only lose most of the new customers, but to probably lose a lot of regular customers in addition, because they cannot get normal service with the new influx of guests. On top of all these woes, you will have spent all that money on advertising for nothing!

Seek Professional Help

When you decide to embark on an advertising and promotion campaign to increase sales and profits, it is wise to get professional help in designing the program best suited for you. Just as you would seek a good lawyer when appearing in court, a good tax specialist when the IRS calls, or a doctor when you are sick, don't attempt to set up your own advertising program. Random advertising, with an ad in the paper and one or two spots on some radio station picked from the yellow pages will not do a good job and often will waste your money. A good advertising agency can study your situation, set up a budget that you can live with, and give you a program that will get you the most for each dollar spent. An agency may tell you that you are not ready to advertise or cannot afford the expenditure, but this is better than wasting a lot of money on hit or miss promotions. These experts have the facts and figures; they can tell you where you should spend that advertising dollar to bring in the most business. You must identify your market or perhaps the market you are trying to reach and let these people take it from there. As someone once said, "He that pleads his own case has a fool for his client!"

SUMMARY

The biggest problem in increasing productivity and sales is to recognize that there is a problem. As a result of years of prosperity and steadily increasing menu prices, the food service industry has been lulled into a false sense of security. People in the industry believe that they are performing at top efficiency, and there is no need to fret and go into a lot of cost saving and waste reduction when it is much easier to just keep raising the prices and enjoy the huge profits. During the days when help was cheap and plentiful, very few even knew what productivity meant, let alone took any steps to increase it. Why worry about such things when you could hire all the people needed for a dollar a day? When there is a cost-increase period (inflation) profits will decrease sharply unless you do one or more of the following:

    Increase selling prices
    Decrease portions and quality
    Increase sales
    Increase productivity
    Cut costs

Naturally the first two on the list are the easiest to do. They will produce the fastest results with the least effort. This is why most people in the industry choose this route, as we can see when we look at current selling prices and the quality of both food and service.

How far you can go with these two easy steps will depend on the public: how much will they tolerate? In inflationary periods all prices and costs are zooming upward; the public learns to accept higher and higher prices while receiving less and less for the money spent. This is why the bottom three solutions on the list are employed only as a last resort. When an increase in the minimum wage was announced, the food service industry immediately announced how much the higher wages would increase costs and exactly how much selling prices would be increased to offset this. There was no mention of increasing sales or productivity, or decreasing other costs and becoming more efficient. The industry instead decided to just pass all of the increases directly along to the consumer. Actually, the wise move for the industry in times of higher costs would be to look into all the possibilities for improving the situation:

Raise prices cautiously
Reduce all costs as much as possible
Eliminate waste
Decrease pilferage
Increase productivity
Increase sales

This program may not produce the overnight results of huge price increases and portion cutting, but in the long run the results will last and continue to produce good profits. Your correction program must be varied to produce a balanced solution to rising costs and lower profits. Large cuts in man hours (wage cost) are not the answer unless you increase the productivity of the employees so that the ones who are left can carry the load and maintain the business. If you cut too deep, then you will be right back in the little- or no-profit situation.

None of us like to admit that we could be doing a better job. Then too, when the going gets rough we figure something or somebody will do something to correct the situation without disturbing us too much. When you read the phenomenal success stories in the trade magazines about certain food service operations which describe sales in the millions and huge profits, it is hard to come down to earth and realize we should be engaging in research to cut waste and improve efficiency. The time to work on research and development is when business is good, profits are high, and you have the money to spend for study and analysis. When you get in deep trouble, you have no money to spend for things that might get you out of the hole.

There is another side to this picture. We know from repeated studies and surveys that the food service industry ranks among the lowest in productivity, wastes about 30 percent of all the energy it consumes, wastes 25 percent of the man hours it uses and is high on the list in financial failures. It would be hard for anyone to say there isn't room for just a little improvement. You might want to think about another point: Perhaps that place doing three million dollars in sales each year with 15 percent net profit ($450,000) could just as easily do $3.3 million a year with 18 percent net profit ($594,000). What's wrong with $144,000 more in profits? With this much more profit that minimum wage increase would not seem like such a disaster!

The other important consideration in sales and productivity is that the effort put forth to improve both should be a sustained one, not just a one-shot deal. In any business continued success will depend on constant growth and increasing efficiency. Few can doubt the success of companies like Western Electric, IBM, and General Motors. Year after year they continue to grow and earn high profits. However, they continue to spend huge sums of money for research and development so that they can continue to increase sales and profits. The same thing applies to advertising. Why do the largest and most successful companies continue to spend the most year after year for advertising? When you get to be as big and successful as Sears and McDonald's, why not sit back, relax, and enjoy the success instead of spending more money than any other company for advertising? The answer is simple: If they didn't advertise and constantly strive to do better, they would not be as large and successful as they are. Years ago the largest manufacturer of cigarettes decided that since they were number one there was no need to spend all that money for advertising when they could add it to the profits. So they drastically cut the advertising budget, soon fell way down from their position as the top company, and never recovered. Earlier, we set a basic rule for increasing productivity:

- Increase sales using the same man hours
- Decrease man hours maintaining same sales
- Increase sales and decrease man hours at the same time

The "EWO" (easy way out) is to either raise menu prices sharply or fire a lot of employees to cut the payroll. It is doubtful whether either of these will produce lasting results. The smart approach is to select the third solution. You should set up weekly and yearly goals for both increased sales and decreased man hours. By constantly increasing your efficiency you can gradually cut man hours and keep your wage cost in line.

Instead of the usual sharp menu price increases, try moderate increases over a longer period of time, coupled with the other ways set forth to increase sales and profits. Once you are on this program, stay on it and keep the profits in line. The situation is something like the average American and dieting. We go along eating everything in sight, then get on the scale and decide we must lose 30 pounds on a crash diet. We lose the 30 pounds and, presto, are back to the groaning board until the 30 pounds are back again. If we stayed on a moderate and sensible diet constantly, there would be no need for the crash diet. The real solution is to get on that scale regularly, recognize that we are slowly gaining weight, and start corrective action early. The same applies to productivity and sales in the food service industry. We must keep "getting on those scales," recognize that we are not as efficient as we could be, and start a continuing program of improvement. Don't wait until the profits are down to little or nothing and then frantically grab for a crash solution. You'll find it much easier to cut the fat a little at a time and see that it does not return.

APPENDIX

Planning and operating food service facilities have become increasingly complex and diverse in recent years. With the invention of new equipment, the increasing use of convenience and prefabricated foods, and the need for techniques to combat rising costs, professional advice is more important than ever.

If you are planning to remodel or open up a new food service operation and would like some consulting help, the following organization has branches all over the world. They offer professional help to anyone, anywhere. If you need help, don't hesitate to contact them. The consultants affiliated with this organization are experienced, qualified, professional food facility designers, planners, and consultants who can help you with your individual problems; they are people who are not engaged in the manufacture, sale, or promotion of food service equipment or supplies.

Following are the geographical locations of this organization.

FOODSERVICE CONSULTANTS SOCIETY INTERNATIONAL
1800 Pickwick Avenue
Glenview, Illinois 60025

Geographical Locations
U.S.A.

Alabama
Alaska
Arizona
Arkansas
California
Colorado
Connecticut
District of Columbia
Florida
Georgia
Illinois
Indiana
Iowa
Kansas
Kentucky
Louisiana
Maryland
Massachusetts

Michigan
Minnesota
Missouri
Nebraska
New Hampshire
New Jersey
New York
North Carolina
Ohio
Oklahoma
Oregon
Pennsylvania
South Carolina
Tennessee
Texas
Virginia
Washington
Wisconsin

Foreign Countries

American Samoa
Canada
Chile
England
France
Germany
Greece
India

Israel
Norway
Philippines
Puerto Rico
Spain
Sweden
Switzerland
Venezuela